HOW TO BUILD
KITCHEN CABINETS
ROOM DIVIDERS and
CABINET FURNITURE

DONALD R. BRANN

Library of Congress Card No. 78-129277

EIGHTH PRINTING — 1976
REVISED EDITION

Published by
DIRECTIONS SIMPLIFIED, INC.

Division of
**EASI-BILD PATTERN CO., INC.
Briarcliff Manor, N.Y. 10510**

TABLE OF CONTENTS

Living Is Doing

Building kitchen cabinets may not, at first glance, appear to be a logical way to find peace of mind, but those who seek release from everyday tensions, soon discover spare time and effort can pay rich rewards. This is easy to understand when one realizes the brain, like muscles and tendons, requires constant flexing to remain strong and healthy.

Just reading this book, learning how the work is done, stimulates the mind. Make an effort, build cabinets your kitchen requires and you obtain hours of complete relaxation, while you economically solve a costly problem.

This book tells how to modernize a kitchen with the different cabinets required. It explains how to build a free standing island, cabinets for sink, drop-in counter range, refrigerator enclosure and wall oven. Step-by-step directions and assembly illustrations explain every step, simplify building cabinets to size specified, or to size space requires. Those who read, discover how designer styled cabinets can be built for only cost of materials.

Learning to modernize a kitchen, like learning to ride a bicycle or drive a car, invariably frightens the beginner. Since only one saw cut or one hole is made at one time, if you make a mistake, there's no great loss. For your effort you gain a handsome reward, a modern kitchen at an incredibly low cost.

Being an individual, one willing to try new ventures, is the key to a fuller life. Don't let anyone "con" you into thinking it can't be done. Try doing and you'll start living.

Don Brann

TO BUILD DESIGNER STYLED CABINETS

This book explains how to build cabinets that can be finished any way you like. If you prefer prefinished hardwood paneled cabinets that require no on the job finishing, recess framing ¼" as step-by-step directions specify.

If you want to antique, paint or wallpaper cabinets, or apply designer styled moldings, use ⅜" flakeboard on ends; recess framing ⅜" where ¼" recess is specified for ¼" plywood, note page 32. Use ¾" flakeboard for doors.

If you want to finish cabinets with colorful carefree plastic laminate doors, bond laminate to both sides of ⅝" flakeboard, or purchase plastic laminate already bonded to flakeboard.

NOTE: Directions allow ¼" recess for ¼" panels. This allows panels to finish flush with legs. If ⅜" flakeboard, or plastic laminate bonded to flakeboard is substituted, recess framing to allow same to finish flush with legs. The only exception is where a cabinet butts against a wall. In this case, follow directions outlined and fasten leg flush with end of framing. All metric dimensions shown are approximate. Note page 98.

Every Kitchen is Different...

A well planned kitchen must fill your family's needs today, and in the future. Since it is used more than any other room and requires more time and energy to operate, everything should be placed within convenient reach. Before doing any work, and before buying any materials or equipment, read this book through completely. Note each illustration when mentioned.

Because kitchens vary in size, shape and location of equipment, and each contains a different combination of windows and doors, place a checkmark alongside each paragraph and illustration that refers to your kitchen. This permits ready reference when you start actual work.

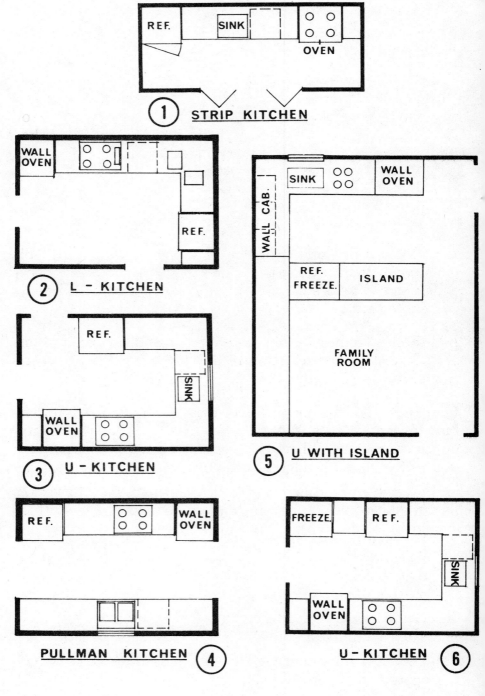

STRIP KITCHEN ①

L - KITCHEN ②

U - KITCHEN ③

PULLMAN KITCHEN ④

U WITH ISLAND ⑤

U - KITCHEN ⑥

SELECT A PRACTICAL PLAN

No special skill or experience is required to transform space into a labor saving kitchen that's a delight to live with. Nor need the job be expensive. Illus. 1, 2, 3, 4, 5, and 6 show basic types of kitchens.

Illus. 1 is ideal for a narrow room. Installation of cabinets is easy and economical. Food from refrigerator is placed on counter, washed in sink, placed on range. The range, flanked by counters, encourages a natural flow of work.

Illus. 2 shows an L-shaped kitchen.

Illus. 3, U-shaped.

A corridor-type along two walls is shown in Illus. 4. In this installation the center aisle should not be less than four feet wide. This provides an economical plan since there are no corners to turn.

A U-shaped kitchen, with free standing island, is shown in Illus. 5. If you install a freezer, allow 18″ to 24″ counter space between freezer and refrigerator, Illus. 6.

Plan like a "pro." Proper distance between appliances is important for two reasons. When too far apart you take too many unnecessary steps. When too close, there isn't enough counter space. If you are considering a complete modernization job, relocate refrigerator, freezer, sink and range according to these recommendations.

1. For greatest efficiency, distance between refrigerator and sink, Illus. 1, should be approximately four feet, not more than eight feet. Distance between sink and range, four to six feet. Between range and refrigerator, four to ten feet.

2. Allow a minimum of three feet passage for door, Illus. 2.

3. Allow 4 ft. minimum clearance when placing a base cabinet opposite an appliance, Illus. 3.

4. If you want to remove an existing door or window, or install one in another location, directions on page 52 explain framing.

5. Avoid placing refrigerator where its door conflicts with a kitchen door. Buy refrigerator with door opening towards sink, Illus. 1. Allow space refrigerator manufacturer recommends for door opening, ventilation. Provide as much counter space as possible on door-opening side of refrigerator, never less than 18″, two to three feet is handy.

6. Provide counter space on both sides of sink and range.

7. While sinks are traditionally placed beneath a window, a counter under window is just as convenient. Never place a range beneath a window.

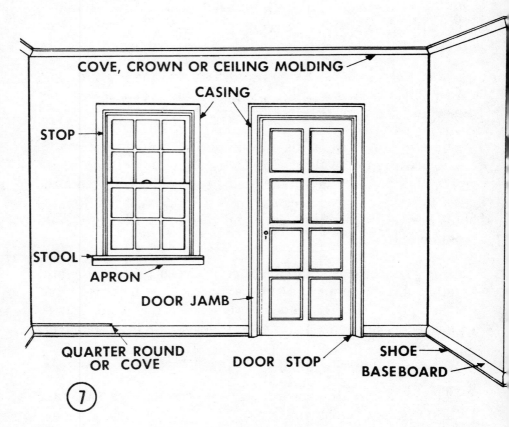

COVE, CROWN OR CEILING MOLDING

CASING

STOP

STOOL

APRON

DOOR JAMB

QUARTER ROUND OR COVE

DOOR STOP

SHOE

BASEBOARD

7

Illus. 7 indicates trim found in most rooms. Since we refer to each by name, note terms used. When estimating space available, always measure from a corner and work out.

Base cabinets are 24″ in depth, Illus. 8. Countertop measures 25″. Allow 15″ to 18″ between bottom of wall cabinet and countertop. Space cabinets above range, distance manufacturer recommends.

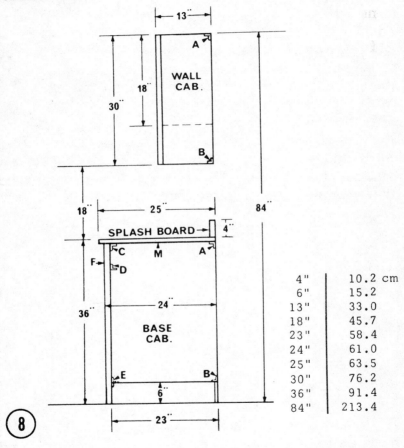

4″	10.2 cm
6″	15.2
13″	33.0
18″	45.7
23″	58.4
24″	61.0
25″	63.5
30″	76.2
36″	91.4
84″	213.4

While most base cabinets, sinks, and countertop ranges, are placed 36″ from floor, a smaller person finds 30″ or 32″ height, more comfortable. It's important to remember the resale value of your house depends heavily on the kitchen. For this reason, a 36″ counter height is a better investment. Install wall oven at height manufacturer recommends.

Measure out 24″ from wall, not baseboard, draw a chalk line on floor, Illus. 9. This line represents face of base cabinet (counter-top projects 1″ beyond). The baseboard and shoe molding Illus. 7, need not be removed but most pros do remove same within area of base cabinets. If baseboard isn't removed, and it has a cove or quarter round molding on top, remove same. If you plan on paneling balance of kitchen, use ³⁄₁₆″ or ¼″ prefinished hard-wood panels. In this case, remove old baseboard, cut a new base 6″ wide from matching paneling.

After drawing outline of floor plan, Illus. 9, indicate radiators, registers, pipes, wall protrusions. Radiators and/or registers should be concealed without impairing their efficiency. Indicate windows with a double line, direction doors swing, etc. Indicate position of equipment, either in present or new position. Next draw a wall plan, Illus. 10 and note location of windows, doors, and equipment. If a new sink is to be installed under a window, check distance D. 40″ height to bottom of window sill allows for a 4″ back splasher, Illus. 11.

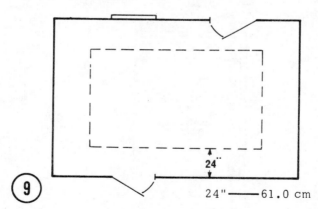

9

24″ ———— 61.0 cm

If window sill is less than 40″, it's still possible to install equipment by following directions on page 51. Measure wall space available from edge of door or window casing. Measure width of window, door, etc. Double check all measurements to make certain you know how much space is available. If you don't move sink, range, refrigerator, etc., take measurements 36″ from floor, also at top of baseboard, Illus. 11. Double check all measurements. Does B plus C equal A?

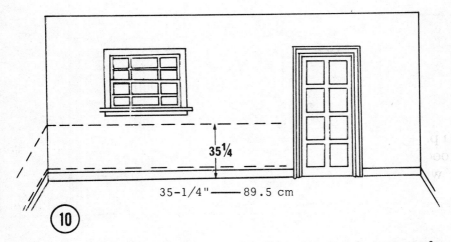

35¼

35-1/4"——— 89.5 cm

(10)

After you have drawn a rough plan, the next step is to transfer plan to ruled paper, page 97. Consider each square one foot of floor space. If a wall measures 8 ft., the same wall drawn on ruled paper would be exactly eight squares wide, Illus. 12. Draw a line across part of a square if it's necessary to indicate inches. If equipment you own or buy, differs in size, draw in exact size. Your appliance dealer or utility company will supply dimensions for equipment selected. Using equipment templates, page 99, draw in each piece. When your scaled sketch indicates location of all equipment, recheck space available for base cabinets.

If you plan on installing a new sink, dishwasher, disposal, freezer, refrigerator, automatic ice making machine, larger hot water heater, or moving sink to new location, get an estimate from two or more reliable plumbers. Show plumber floor plan so he can accurately estimate exact amount of material required. Get an estimate for materials and equipment separate from labor. This permits doing a modernization job piecemeal if desired. If plumber suggests moving sink to save fittings, or labor, follow his suggestion providing it doesn't eliminate required counter space. If a dishwasher, clothes washer or disposal is to be installed, ask plumber to check capacity of hot water heater and waste line. Call your building inspector to confirm size of waste line required before buying equipment. In some areas installation of an additional piece of equipment may require new and larger waste line.

13

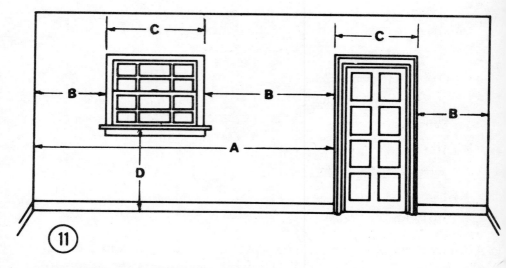

ADD NEEDED OUTLETS

A modern kitchen requires many wall outlets, ample lighting, separate service lines for dishwasher, disposal, wall oven, range, air conditioner, hot water heater, etc. Moving a range to new location need not be costly. Actual expense can be figured by cost of additional gas pipe or cable, plus time required to connect. In some cases a new range, wall oven and refrigerator, can be connected to your present service lines. If a new range is placed in approximately same location as old one, it's frequently possible to use existing outlet with a new range cord. Book #694 Electrical Repairs Simplified explains how to install a new range outlet.

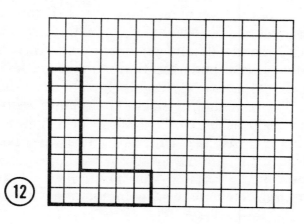

14

Check List
GAS

☐ Gas Range or Wall Oven and
Surface Cooking Unit

☐ Refrigerator

☐ Hot Water Heater

☐ Washer-Dryer

☐ Incinerator

☐ Room Heater

ELECTRIC

☐ Kitchen overhead light

☐ Light over Sink

☐ Lights under Wall Cabinets

☐ Island Outlet

☐ Outdoor flood light

☐ Ventilating fan

☐ Air Conditioner *

Wall Outlets for:

☐ Refrigerator

☐ Washing Machine *

☐ Home Freezer *

☐ Clock

☐ Coffee Maker, Knife Sharpener, Mixer, Toaster, Radio, and similar kitchen appliances.

110 volt separate circuit wiring for:

☐ Dishwasher   ☐ Disposer   ☐ Ironer

220 volt, 3 wire service for:

☐ Washer-Dryer   ☐ Electric Range or Wall Oven and Surface Cooking Unit

(13)

* Separate circuit advisable

Many new appliances require separate service lines, Illus. 13. Go over this check list and note changes you want to make. Add all your other wiring needs. Mark location of proposed switches and outlets on plan. This careful planning enables the electrician to give you a more accurate estimate based on materials and labor. Ask your electrician to recheck location of each outlet to make certain it is placed in a convenient location.

If you plan on installing an air conditioner, be sure a separate line is installed or outlet you plan on using provides necessary wattage.

Visit your utility company. Tell them what new appliances you plan on adding. They will advise whether present service is adequate to serve all equipment. Call the telephone company and ask them to install a line to the kitchen.

Be sure to install one or more outlets in the side or top of a free standing island. Also install wiring for garage door opener.

BUY APPLIANCES

While appliances can be purchased at almost any price, the cheapest is seldom the best investment. An established dealer, who sells at prices recommended by manufacturer, can help get satisfaction if anything goes wrong. Ask for exact dimensions of equipment selected. Recheck layout to make certain each fits space planned.

PREPARE ROOM

Next prepare room by removing everything possible. Wall space up to 84" should be cleared. If you plan on installing a new sink, range or refrigerator, don't disconnect anything until new equipment is ready for installation.

CHECK FLOOR

If your floor requires recovering, remove old covering. Nail down loose boards. If rough, sand smooth. If too rough, or too springy, cover with ¼" tempered hardboard, or ⅜", ½" or ⅝" — particle board underlayment. This is available in 4x8 panels. Use thickness required to stiffen floor. Nail every 6" along edges, every 8" to 10" along floor joists. Use 6 penny coated box nails.

If floor is firm, but uneven, or slopes slightly, you can smooth, and/or level, with plastic floor underlayment. Plastic underlayment can be spread with a trowel from a feathered edge, to ⁵⁄₁₆″ thick in one coat, and any number of coats can be applied. It dries to a hard base — perfect for ceramic or asphalt tile. Follow manufacturer's directions for applying underlayment selected.

If you plan on carpeting the floor, remove shoe molding.

It is important for equipment and appearance that floor be level. To determine whether floor has any high points, check with a two foot level and straight 2 x 4 at various points along outer edge, Illus. 14. When you find highest point, measure up 35¼″. Using level as a straight edge, Illus. 16, draw a line around room at 35¼″ height. At various points measure down to floor. If any point is less than 35¼″, you didn't select highest point. Start over and draw a new line at 35¼″.

To simplify construction, aluminum is recommended for all framing, prefinished paneling for all cabinets, flakeboard for shelves and doors. Place plywood and flakeboard in room where it is to be used.

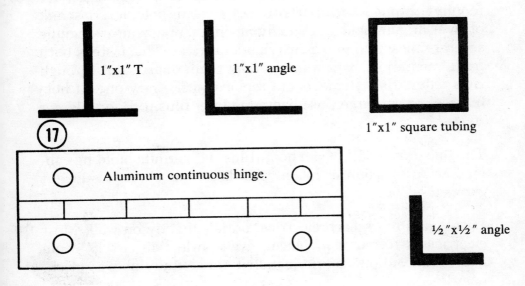

1″x1″ T

1″x1″ angle

1″x1″ square tubing

17

Aluminum continuous hinge.

½″x½″ angle

Illus. 17 shows various shapes of aluminum required.

1"x1" angle; 1"x1" square tubing;
1"x1" T; ½"x½" angle;
Aluminum continuous hinge.

All extrusions are available in six foot, some in eight foot lengths. Buy longest length required. When necessary, butt ends over a stud, or on center of leg. When fastening aluminum to stud in wall, use 1½" big head aluminum roofing nails.

Use drive pins, Illus. 18, for masonry walls.

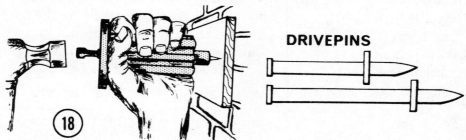

DRIVEPINS

When fastening two parts, use aluminum rivets, Illus. 19. Use size rivet thickness of material requires. Drill hole size rivet requires through both parts. Insert rivet in hole, insert shank of rivet in gun, hold gun snugly against metal, squeeze handle several times until gun snaps shank off rivet. This fastens both parts securely. If you want to take them apart, drill through rivet, Illus. 19A. Remove and replace with a new one. If hole happens to get larger, use back up plate, Illus. 19B, or a larger rivet.

The line drawn 35¼" from floor, Illus. 11, permits building cabinets with 36" counter height. All directions cover this height cabinet.

Locate and mark each electrical outlet directly on wall. Most electricians recommend placing wall outlets 40" to 48" from floor. Wall outlets can be installed horizontally above splashboard.

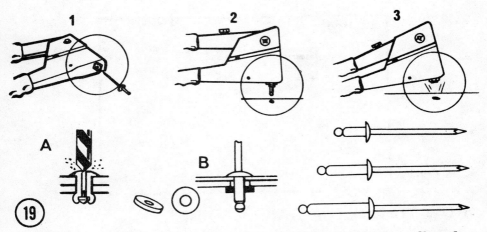

If you want to move the sink, outline new location on wall and floor. This eliminates any question as to location of waste and water lines. Be sure to indicate exact location of freezer, refrigerator, dishwasher, disposal, clothes washer, dryer, etc. Your appliance dealer can give you information concerning size of wire equipment requires, wattage it requires, etc. If the circuit is already loaded with appliances, don't expect it to power additional equipment unless it's fused to supply current required. If you have a spare terminal in your fuse panel it would be better to run a #12 wire circuit. This can be fused with a 20 amp fuse. This will provide 20x120 = 2400 watts up to approximately 30 feet from fuse panel.

Careful planning helps the electrician and plumber rough in lines required.

Allow plumber and electrician to cut required holes through wall, floor or ceiling. Ask plumber to run a snake through waste line to make certain it is completely free before he connects new sink, dishwasher or disposal.

Wall cabinets can be installed to 81″ or 84″ height, Illus. 8. We recommend 84″. Remove old cabinets. Double check your plan and dimensions by drawing each cabinet and piece of equipment full size directly on wall. Use chalk or crayon, Illus. 20. Use a 2 ft. or longer level when you draw outline of cabinets to insure drawing vertical and horizontal lines correctly.

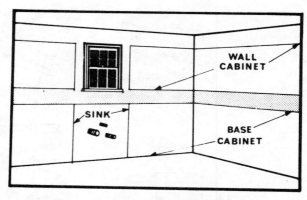

HOW TO BUILD A BASE CABINET

Fasten 1"x1" angle, length required, to wall at 35¼", and 6", or at top of baseboard, Illus. 21. If a wall oven, or refrigerator enclosure is to be built, fasten angle above top of refrigerator or wall oven. Allow space appliance manufacturer recommends. If baseboard is higher than 6", angle can be fastened to top of baseboard. If baseboard is less than 6", fasten angle at 6" height.

Since angle should be fastened to studs in wall, measure 16" from corner and probe with a 4 or 6 penny finishing nail. When you locate a stud, use level to draw vertical lines, Illus. 21.

Locate and drill ⅛" holes in angle. Fasten angle to studs in position shown. If you are building cabinets against a masonry wall, use 1½" drive pins. Fasten 1" angle to wall, in position required for refrigerator, and/or wall oven enclosure, Illus. 21. Butt angle end-to-end over a stud. Another way of fastening end-to-end is shown in Illus. 22. Drill holes and rivet 4" to 6" piece to underside.

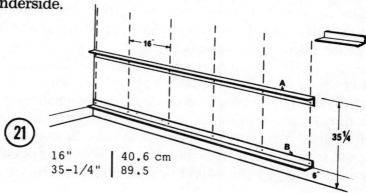

16"	40.6 cm
35-1/4"	89.5

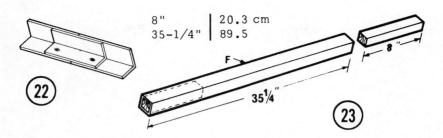

8"   20.3 cm
35-1/4"   89.5

F

35¼"

Cut legs F — 35¼". Use 1" square tubing. Cut ¾ x ⅞ x 8" filler blocks from 1x2. Insert block all the way into both ends, Illus. 23.

NOTE: ¼" panels finish flush with face of legs. Illustrations and directions indicate leg projecting ¼" beyond end of framing. The only exception is where a cabinet butts against a wall. In this case leg is fastened flush with end of framing. Use ¼" prefinished paneling on all exposed cabinet surfaces; ¼" fir plywood, good side facing into cabinet, elsewhere.

Illus. 24 shows location of various parts and indicates what aluminum to use. If you notch 1" angle A at corner, where it meets K, it makes a neat corner. Note KA, Illus. 24. Drill holes and nail A and K to studs.

Illus. 24LB shows position of 1" angle. This provides framing for bottom shelf. If you want an additional shelf part way up, follow same method of framing.

Illus. AG shows how A and G are fastened together with a rivet. Do not notch. Clamp both pieces together, or hold with pliers in exact position required and drill ⅛" hole through both pieces. An electric drill is a must. Insert shaft of a ¼" medium length rivet in hole, shank in tool, squeeze handle several times.

To simplify construction, we suggest spacing legs F in base cabinets, Illus. 24, either two, three or four feet apart. For a four foot cabinet, cut ¾" flakeboard N — 4"x48" and use as a spacer; 4"x24" for a two foot cabinet. Always cut N length required to fit space available, but never longer than 48".

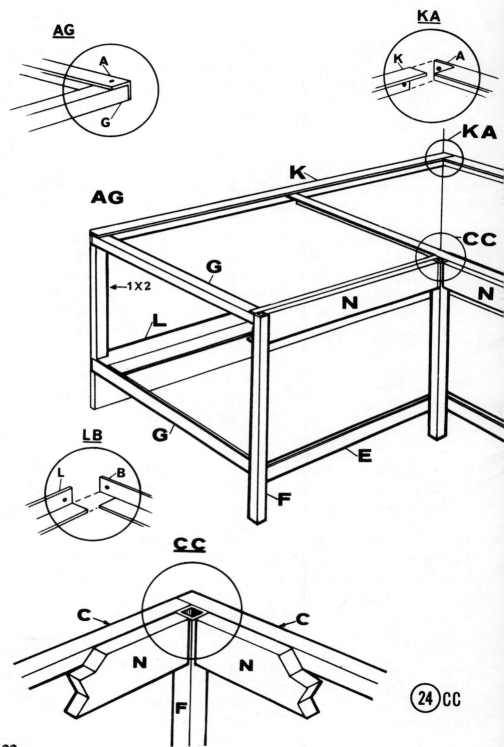

AG

KA

KA

K

AG

CC

G

N

←1X2

N

L

LB

G

L B

G

E

F

CC

C

C

N

N

24 CC

F

A,B,C,D,G,K,L – 1" ANGLE
E – 1" T
F – 1" SQUARE TUBING
N – ¾" FLAKEBOARD

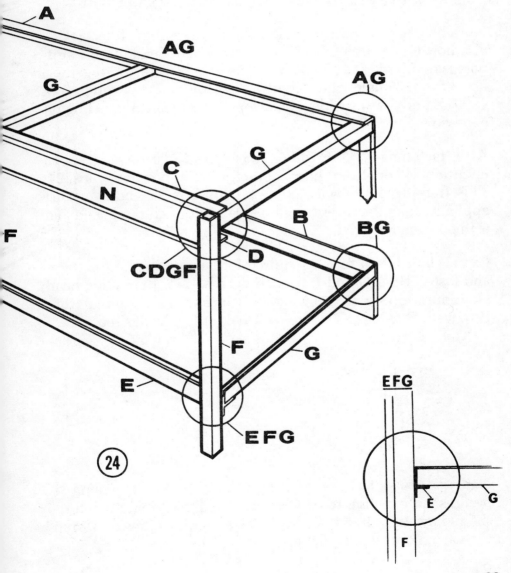

Fasten C flush with top of leg, ¼″ recess permits fastening paneling flush with face of leg. Fasten D — 4″ below top of F. Rivet E to F — 6″, or height from floor B requires. If in doubt as to exact height, place G on B and E, place level on G, fasten E to F in position required, Illus. 26.

Use N to space legs. Drill holes through C and D, fasten C and D to N with ⅝″ No. 10 binding head aluminum screws. Check C and F with a 2 ft. square before fastening D and E to F.

Note how one C projects 1″ beyond leg in corner, Illus. 24CC, also how C can project to K, Illus. 24, when an additional support is required. If you butt two pieces of countertop together, do so over 1″ angle. Since edge of leg projects ¼″ beyond A, B, C, D, E and G it provides space for ¼″ prefinished paneling on exposed ends.

After fastening C, D, E to F; C and D to N, cut G — 22⅞″, to maintain 24″ depth for base cabinet, rivet in position, Illus. 24. This framing permits installing a drop-in sink and range. If appliance manufacturer recommends additional framing, fasten G in position required.

Cut ½″ flakeboard to size required for bottom shelf. Drill holes and fasten B, E, G and L to shelf with ⅝″ No. 10 binding head aluminum screws. If you want a shelf midway, fasten another B to wall, E to legs, G where required, at height desired.

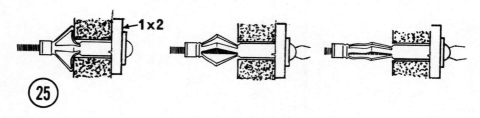

Nail 1x2's to wall, Illus. 24. This permits gluing or nailing ¼″ prefinished paneling to exposed ends of base cabinet. Illus. 25 shows how 1x2 can be fastened to wall with expansion fasteners, when no stud is available.

For counter top M, use ¾"x25" width flakeboard length required, Illus. 26. If it's necessary to butt two pieces together, do
so over a G. Install additional G where required. Flakeboard
comes in a wide variety of widths and lengths ranging from 12"
to 60" wide, 48" to 144" in length.

Cut ¾" flakeboard 4", or width desired, by length required for
backsplash. Most custom kitchen installers cover entire area
between countertop and bottom of wall cabinet with a plastic
laminate backsplash, indicated by shaded area, Illus. 20. Many
building material retailers will prefabricate countertops to exact size your cabinets require.

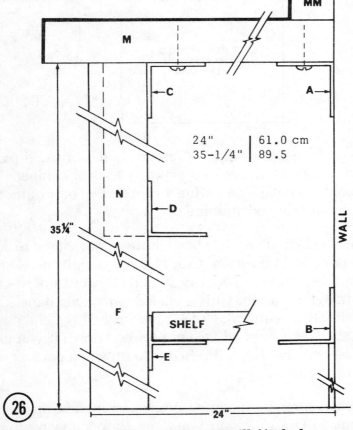

| 24" | 61.0 cm |
| 35-1/4" | 89.5 |

Fasten countertop M in position. Drill ⅛" holes every 12" to
18" through A, K, G, C and fasten to M with ⅝" No. 10 binding
head aluminum screws.

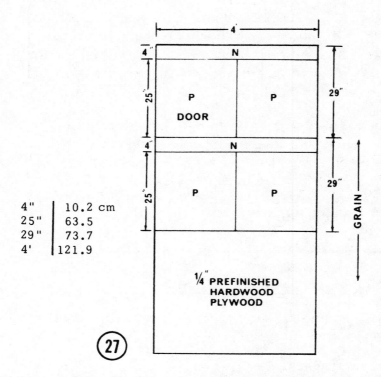

4"	10.2 cm
25"	63.5
29"	73.7
4'	121.9

To insure professional results, ¼" prefinished hardwood paneling is used to face N, doors, and exposed ends of cabinet. Prefinished paneling comes in a wide variety of wood grains that requires no "on the job" staining or waxing.

The cutting chart, Illus. 27, shows how to cut parts to keep grain and pattern in position. Cut 4" strips, length needed for N. Next cut door panels. Identify N and adjacent door panels to insure matching grain. Cut ½" flakeboard door panels 25", Illus. 28, by width required. Cut ¼" prefinished paneling same size, Illus. 29. Keep finished face of plywood down if you use a portable electric saw. Keep finished face up when cutting with a hand or table saw.

Using notched spreader manufacturer recommends, apply contact cement to O and P and bond together following manufacturer's directions. Prime coat, then paint inside face of O using color desired. Apply flexible wood trim to exposed edges of door with white glue.

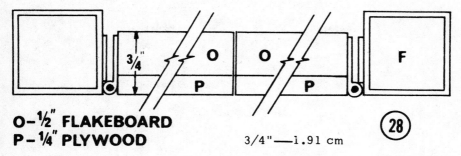

O-½" FLAKEBOARD
P-¼" PLYWOOD

3/4"—1.91 cm

(28)

Cut ¾" continuous hinge 25", or length required. Place hinge flush with face of leg, Illus. 28. Hinge should just clear bottom of N. Mark and drill holes in leg at top and bottom of hinge, Illus. 30. Do not fasten hinge to leg at this time. Fasten hinge to edge of door in position shown, Illus. 28, with ¾" No. 8 flat-head aluminum wood screws. Rivet hinge to leg, then drill additional holes required to fasten hinge securely to F. Illus. 31 shows how doors are hinged to leg in corner.

Fasten magnetic cabinet door catch to top of bottom shelf so it stops and holds door in position required.

PLASTIC LAMINATE APPLICATION

Apply plastic laminate to countertop and backsplash. Plastic laminate is available 24" to 60" in width; lengths up to twelve feet, in a wide variety of colors. Buy width and length counter top and splashboard requires.

Using a square and a soft lead or grease pencil, measure, mark and cut laminate. If you have a radial arm or other table saw, use hollow saw ground blade keeping good face up.

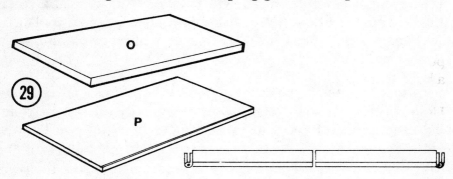

27

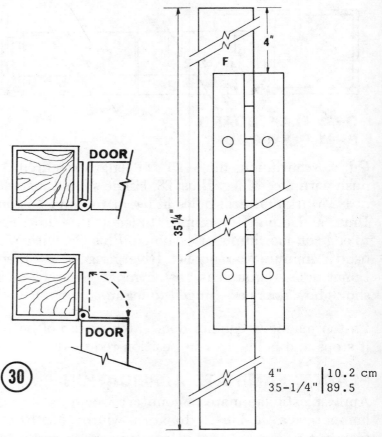

4"	10.2 cm
35-1/4"	89.5

If you cut laminate with a portable electric circular saw, use the special 6½″ blade recommended for plastic laminate. Keep good face down. When using power tools, always note direction blade turns. If it starts cutting at top of laminate, it's cross cutting. Keep good face up. If blade starts cutting at bottom, it's ripping. Keep good face down. Try a piece of scrap and you'll quickly appreciate how to cut laminate using power tools. Always cut on outside of line. This permits filing or planing edge to size required.

Plastic laminate can be cut with a fine tooth crosscut handsaw or keyhole saw. Keep good face up. Saw only on down stroke. To keep from chipping, clamp laminate between two boards, Illus. 32. Always cut laminate oversize to permit filing or planing edge to size required.

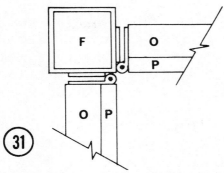

Following manufacturer's directions, apply contact cement to flakeboard countertop and to plastic laminate. When cement has been allowed to set period prescribed by manufacturer, apply second coat. Bond plastic laminate to countertop. File or plane edge to size required. Cut ¾″ flakeboard backsplash. Apply laminate to backsplash. Saw cutouts where required for outlet boxes. Your plastic laminate dealer has a wide selection of moldings that can be used to finish edge of counter and backsplash.

DROP-IN SINK AND RANGE CABINET

Ask your plumber and electrician if they will make cutout for sink and range. If they suggest that you do it, ask them to locate exact position. Draw outline for drop-in sink and range using full size templates supplied by appliance retailer. A saber saw blade with 10 teeth to the inch simplifies sawing cutout.

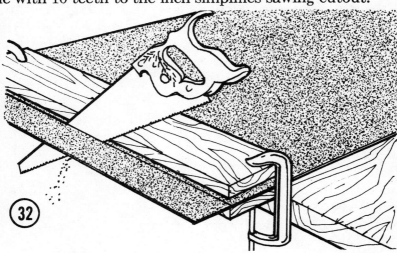

Drill ¼″ holes on inside of line, Illus. 33. Cut opening. Opening can also be cut with a metal cutting keyhole saw. Since rim on sink or range covers opening, it's unnecessary to file edge of opening. Fasten sink and range in position with rim and clamps manufacturer provides. Drill holes or make cutouts for faucets, or control panel, where same is required.

Cut prefinished panels size required. Apply white glue and brad in position to exposed ends.

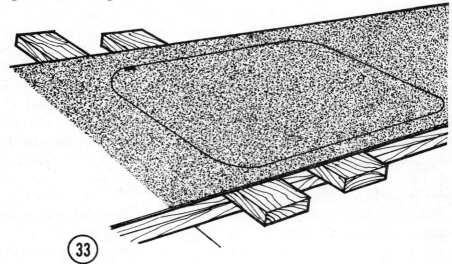

(33)

WALL CABINET

Wall cabinet construction follows this procedure. Cut ¼″ fir plywood back 30″ (for 30″ high cabinet) by width space requires, less ½″, Illus. 34. Directions suggest building cabinets 13″ in depth. They can be built any other size. We specify 13″ since it meets all requirements and provides an economical cutting of material. Wherever possible, build wall cabinets to width that matches base cabinet. The only exception may be over a sink or range where two narrow cabinets, Illus. 40, can be installed to allow more headroom.

A wall cabinet consists of ¼″ plywood back, top, two ends; metal specified, shelves and doors, Illus. 37. Use ¼″ fir plywood, good face in, for back, and ends that butt against a wall; use ¼″ pre-finished on exposed ends.

30

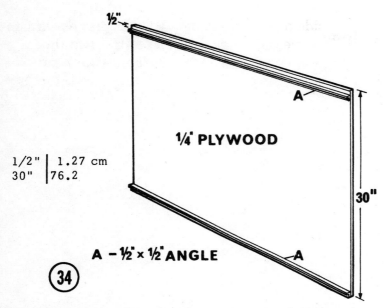

½"

¼" PLYWOOD

1/2" | 1.27 cm
30" | 76.2

30"

A – ½" × ½" ANGLE

A

A

(34)

Cut ½" angle, to length equal to back panel. Cut legs F from 1" square tubing full height of cabinet. Clamp ½" angle in position to back, ½" down from top, Illus. 34; another flush with bottom. Drill ⅛" holes every 10" to 12" through metal and plywood. Rivet through back into metal. This places smooth side of rivet against plywood.

Fasten E ¼" in from edge of F, Illus. 35, 36, with two rivets. Use a piece of ¼" plywood scrap as a spacer.

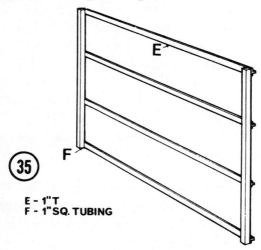

E

F

(35)

E - 1" T
F - 1" SQ. TUBING

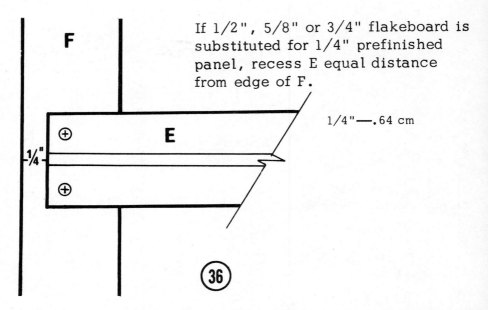

If 1/2", 5/8" or 3/4" flakeboard is substituted for 1/4" prefinished panel, recess E equal distance from edge of F.

1/4"—.64 cm

(36)

For shelves up to 36″ in length, cut ½″ flakeboard 11⅝″ wide by length required; use ⅝″ thick on longer or wider shelves. Cut shelves same length as A and E. Drill holes and fasten E to bottom of shelf with ½″ No. 6 binding head aluminum screws, Illus. 38. Cut ¼″ plywood ends 12″x30″.

Using square, draw outline of shelves on ends. Illus. 39. Nail 1 x 2 across shelves to hold square. Apply glue and nail ends to shelves with 4 penny finishing nails spaced every 3″. Apply glue and nail back to shelves with 4 penny box nails every 4″ to 6″. Nail ends to back. Plane edge of end flush with back. Build doors full length of F. Hinge doors following procedure previously outlined. Countersink nailheads and fill holes.

Secure cabinets to wall 18″, or height desired above counter, by screwing through back, and/or end, into studs. If back of cabinet can't be fastened to two or more studs, use screw anchors, note page 24.

18″ clearance above counter is considered satisfactory except over sink and range. An 18″ high cabinet over sink provides 30″ headroom; a 24″ cabinet allows 24″. Follow range manufacturer's recommendations when placing cabinets over range.

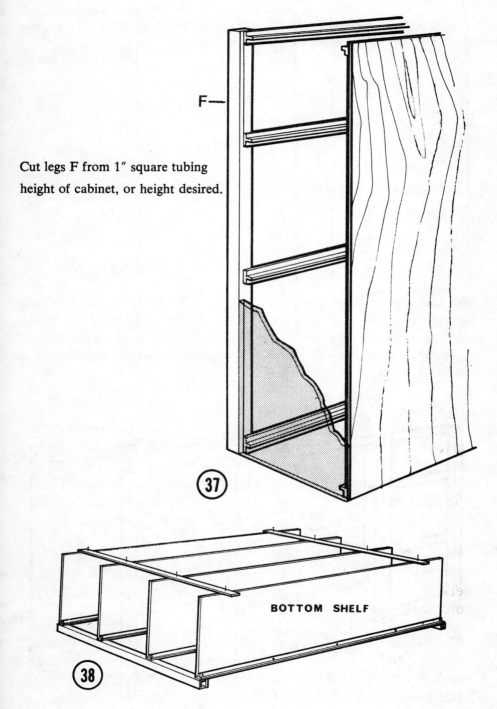

Cut legs F from 1″ square tubing height of cabinet, or height desired.

F—

(37)

BOTTOM SHELF

(38)

33

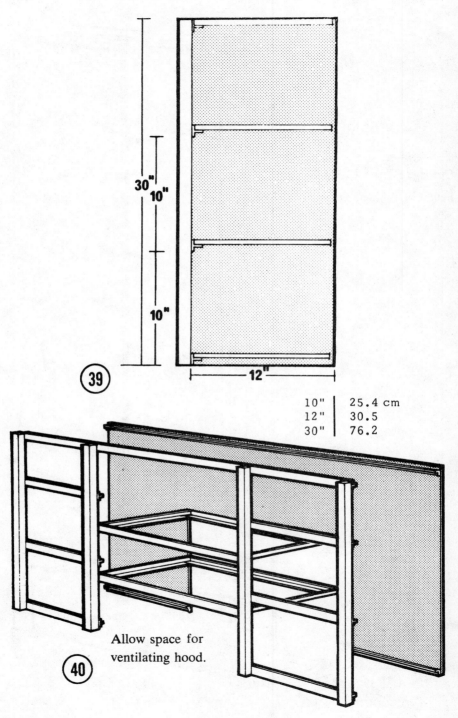

30"
10"
10"
10"

12"

10"	25.4 cm
12"	30.5
30"	76.2

39

40 Allow space for ventilating hood.

34

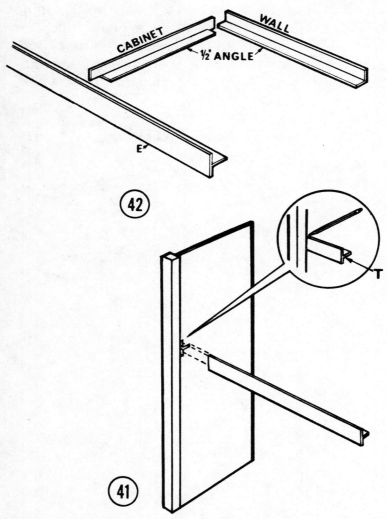

If you want to connect cabinets over a sink or range with shelves, or a narrow cabinet, Illus. 40, cut ¼″ plywood back to size and shape required. Cut plywood for outside ends 12″; cut inside ends, those adjacent to sink, 11¾″ wide. Use 1″ T across front, ½″ angle on sides and across back. Mark and cut shape of T in plywood end, Illus. 41. Rivet E to F in position desired. Cut ½″ angle fastened to cabinet, shape shown, Illus. 42, when butting angle to T, angle to angle. Use ½″ or ⅝″ flakeboard for shelving. Fasten cabinet to wall by screwing through plywood into studs.

REFRIGERATOR ENCLOSURE

An enclosure for a refrigerator can be built as a free-standing unit with four legs, Illus. 43, or as a built-in. When refrigerator is placed against wall, build it in. If refrigerator is part of an island, or separates kitchen from dining area, make it free standing. Space legs width manufacturer recommends, Illus. 44.

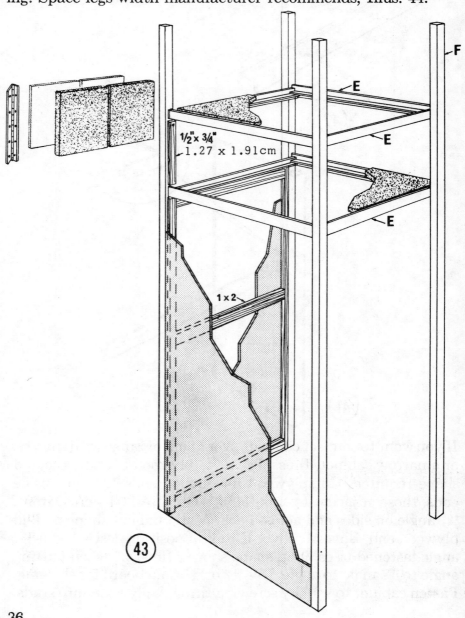

½" x ¾"
1.27 x 1.91cm

1 x 2

43

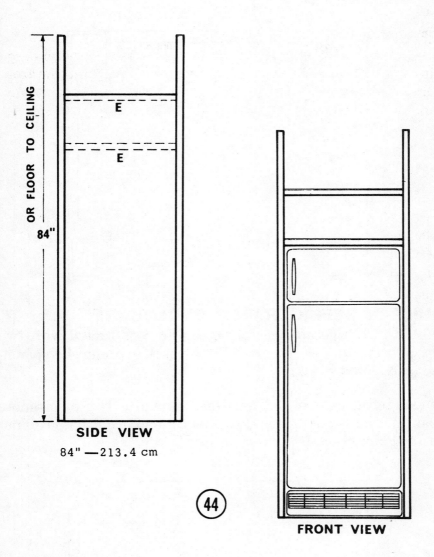

OR FLOOR TO CEILING

84"

SIDE VIEW

84" —213.4 cm

(44)

FRONT VIEW

FREE STANDING CABINET

Cut 4 legs. Rivet 1″ T in position for shelf, at height above refrigerator manufacturer recommends. Screw ½″ x ¾″ strips, cut from 1x2, Illus. 45, wherever ¼″ plywood sides require same. You can stiffen plywood with 1x2 as shown, Illus. 43. Area above refrigerator can be open shelves or enclosed with hinged doors.

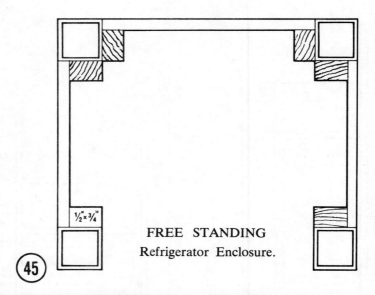

FREE STANDING
Refrigerator Enclosure.

45

BUILT-IN REFRIGERATOR ENCLOSURE

A built-in refrigerator enclosure can be constructed with two legs in front, Illus. 46. Fasten 1″ T to legs. Use prefinished paneling on exposed sides.

Since a refrigerator or wall oven enclosure usually projects more than 24″ from wall, fasten door hinge on adjacent base cabinet to a 1x1 aluminum leg or to a strip of ½″ x ¾″.

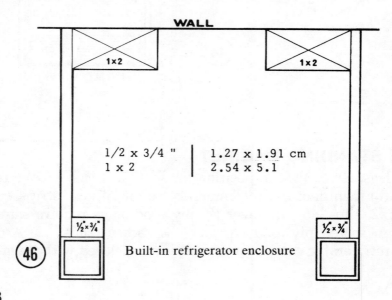

| 1/2 x 3/4 " | 1.27 x 1.91 cm |
| 1 x 2 | 2.54 x 5.1 |

46 Built-in refrigerator enclosure

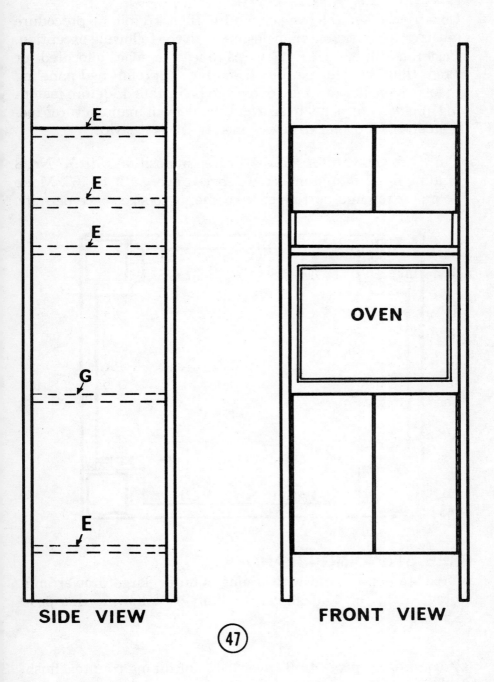

SIDE VIEW

OVEN

FRONT VIEW

(47)

WALL OVEN ENCLOSURE

Construction of wall oven enclosure, Illus. 47, follows procedure outlined for refrigerator enclosure, with the following exception. Fasten additional ½″ x ¾″ strips to legs, in space allocated for oven, Illus. 48. This permits fastening ¼″ prefinished paneling to face of enclosure where oven is to be installed. Before fastening in place, cut panel to size and shape oven manufacturer recommends. Or oven can be fastened to ½″ x ¾″ strips.

Cut ¾″ flakeboard for shelves. Fasten in position with ¾″ No. 8 binding head aluminum screws spaced every 12″ to 16″. Make doors for top and bottom compartments to size space permits.

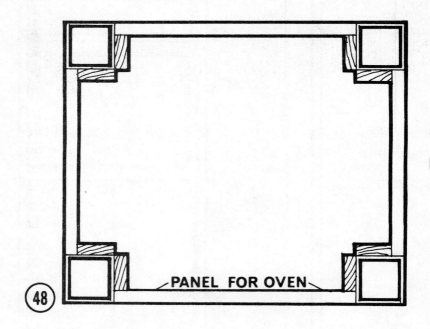

PANEL FOR OVEN

48

FREE STANDING ISLAND

A free standing island with dining counter, large drawer and storage area, Illus. 49-56, can be built by following this procedure.

32″ countertop projects 6″ over back for dining counter, flush on drawer side.

6″

Cut legs F 35¼″. Insert filler blocks. To insure fastening drawer guides accurately, make a 26″ x 35¼″, inside dimension, layout jig, Illus. 50, using 1x2 and panel. Use a square to check corners. Place legs in position, hold with 1x2 blocks, Illus. 51. Cut 1″ angle 25½″ for H. Notch at both ends, Illus. 52. Rivet H 1″ below top of F, in position shown. Cut three E and one HH 25½″. Do not notch HH.

To insure spacing drawer slides E and H proper distance apart, cut ½″ flakeboard for drawer sides. Fasten H and E in position shown, Illus. 54, or cut drawer sides 1/16″ less in width and use side as spacer, Illus. 53. Insert two 4 penny finishing nails between E and side. Fasten E snugly in position. This provides clearance required.

Follow same procedure when fastening other drawer glides in position. Don't fasten HH, Illus. 54, in position at this time. You can fasten ½″ x ¾″ glue blocks, Illus. 55, in position between EH, EE, or do it after frame has been assembled. We suggest doing it later as you will then appreciate where same is required.

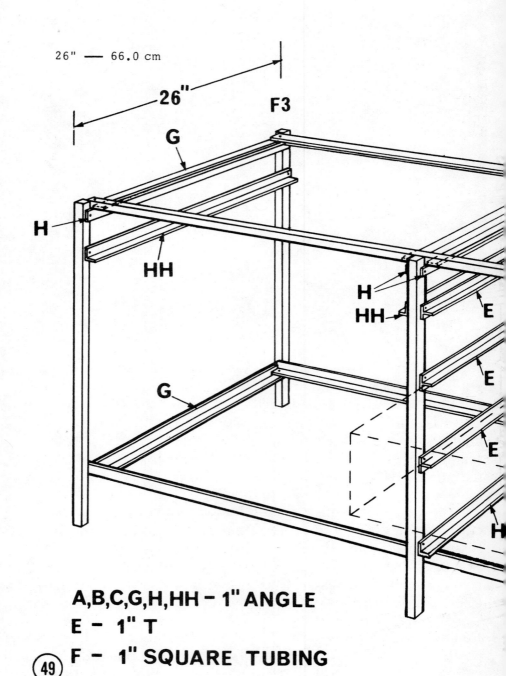

26" — 66.0 cm

26"

F3

G

H

HH

H

HH

E

E

E

G

H

A,B,C,G,H,HH – 1" ANGLE
E – 1" T
F – 1" SQUARE TUBING

49

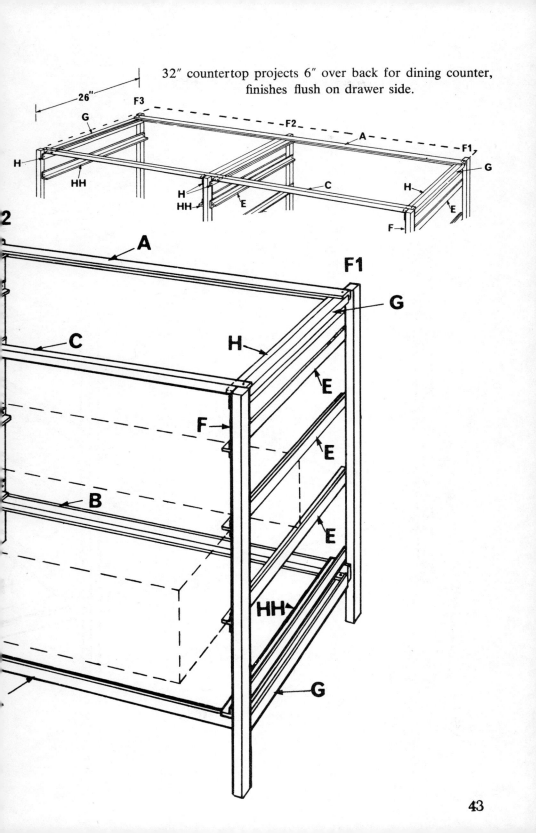

32″ countertop projects 6″ over back for dining counter, finishes flush on drawer side.

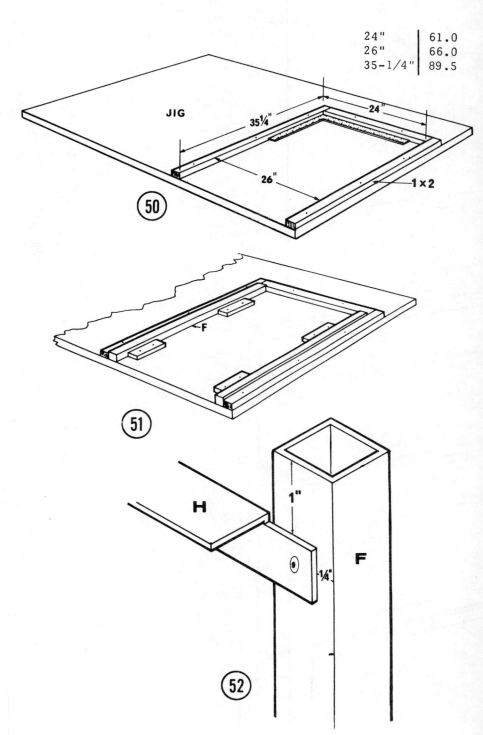

24"	61.0
26"	66.0
35-1/4"	89.5

JIG

35¼"

24"

26"

1 x 2

(50)

F

(51)

H

1"

¼"

F

(52)

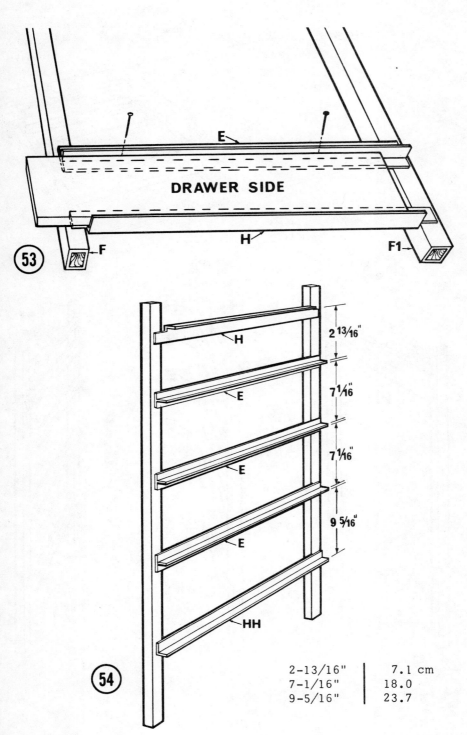

DRAWER SIDE

E

F

H

F1

53

H

E $2^{13}\!/_{16}$"

E $7^{1}\!/_{16}$"

E $7^{1}\!/_{16}$"

E $9^{5}\!/_{16}$"

HH

54

2–13/16"	7.1 cm
7–1/16"	18.0
9–5/16"	23.7

45

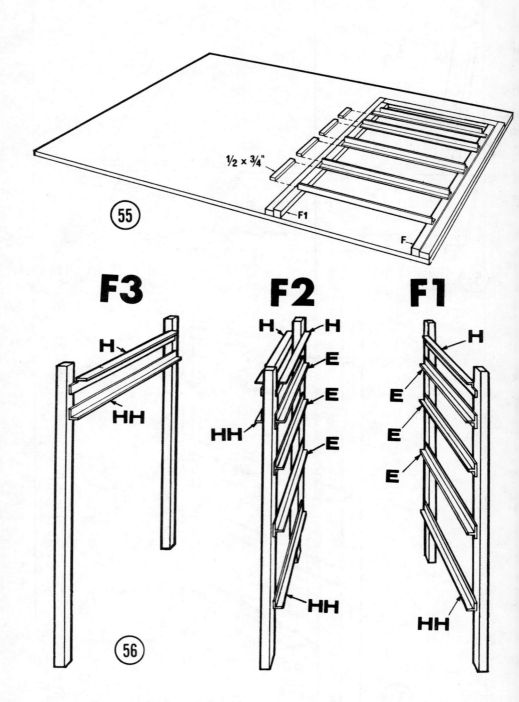

½ × ¾"

F1

F.

⑤⑤

F3

H

HH

F2

H   H

E

E

HH

E

HH

F1

H

E

E

E

HH

⑤⑥

H, HH – 1" ANGLE
E – 1" T

46

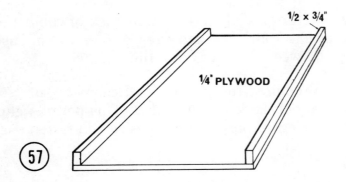

57

Remove frame F-1 from jig and build another for F-2, Illus. 56. Cut ¼″ plywood 24″x27″, Illus. 57. Glue and nail plywood to ½″x¾″ blocks. Screw partition in position, Illus. 58. Fasten H in position to storage area side of Frame F-2. Build frame F-3 following same procedure.

Rivet ABCE, Illus. 49, in position ¼″ in from edge of leg. Keep A and C flush with top of leg. Cut G length required. G is fastened in position flush with ends of ABCE. Rivet A to G, C to G, B to G, E to G. Cut ¾″ flakeboard to size required for bottom shelf. Drill holes and fasten in position with ¾″ No. 8 binding head screws. Rivet HH in position.

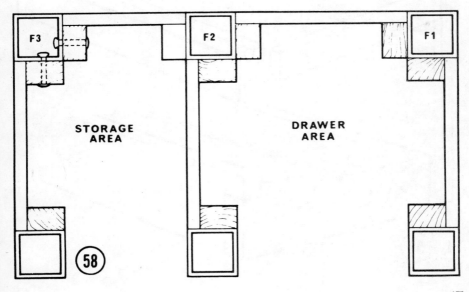

58

To simplify fastening panels to ends and back of cabinet, cut ½" x ¾" glue blocks from 1"x2" and screw or rivet to leg. Fasten blocks to legs between drawer glides, Illus. 55, 58.

Cut panels size required to cover back of cabinet. Cut ¾"x1" strip width required, fasten to A and B. This permits gluing panels flush with legs. Apply panel adhesive and fasten panels in position.

DRAWER CONSTRUCTION

Illus. 59 shows construction of drawers. Cut sides of top drawer 2¾" x 22¾", or size required, from ½" plywood. Cut back 2¾" by width required from ¾" plywood. Cut front 3¾" from ¾" plywood. Since sides nail into back and front, to estimate width of back, measure overall width of opening, deduct 1" for sides, ⅛" for spacing. This provides 1/16" clearance on each side. Notch front ½" deep by 1" as shown, Illus. 60.

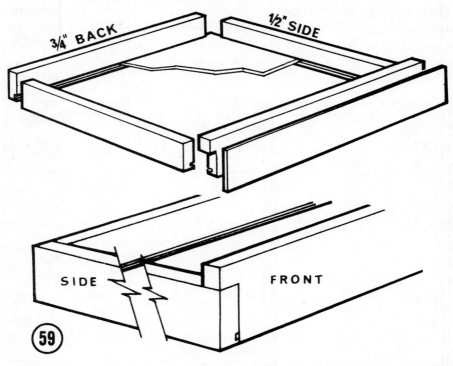

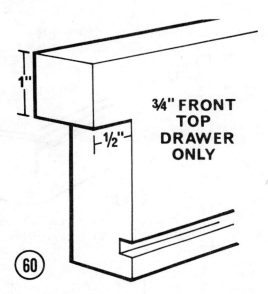

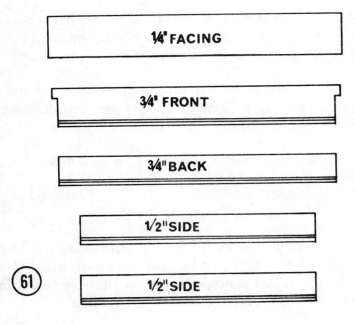

3/4" FRONT
TOP
DRAWER
ONLY

1"

1/2"

60

Using an electric or hand saw, saw ¼″ rabbet, ³⁄₁₆″ deep, ¼″ from bottom. Cut ¼″ plywood to size required, apply white glue to rabbet, to ends of front and back, insert bottom in rabbet, nail sides to front and back with 6 penny finishing nails. Cut ¼″ prefinished paneling for facing 4″, by width of front, plus ½″. Facing projects ¼″ beyond both sides and ¼″ below, Illus. 61.

1/4" FACING

3/4" FRONT

3/4" BACK

1/2" SIDE

61

1/2" SIDE

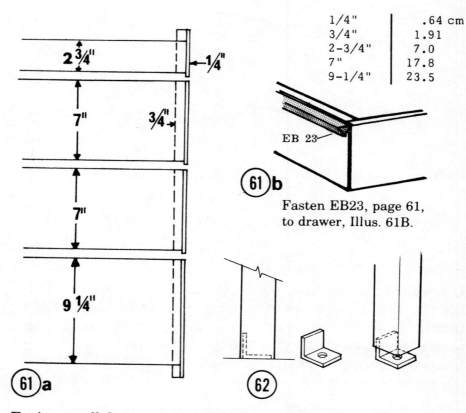

1/4"	.64 cm
3/4"	1.91
2-3/4"	7.0
7"	17.8
9-1/4"	23.5

Fasten EB23, page 61, to drawer, Illus. 61B.

Facing on all drawers project ¼" beyond sides, ¼" below, except on bottom drawer where it projects 1". The ¼" projection acts as a stop. Cut facing to size opening permits.

Build doors for storage area following directions previously outlined. Install magnetic door catch, drawer and door hardware following manufacturers' directions.

As previously suggested, paint inside face of all doors.

Using white glue, fasten flexible wood trim to all exposed edges. Cut edge after glue has been allowed to set.

If you want to anchor legs F to floor, do not use a filler block, Illus. 62. Cut a piece of angle just large enough to fit into bottom of leg. Drill hole and fasten angle to floor with drive tool. Place leg over angle, drill hole; rivet or screw leg to angle.

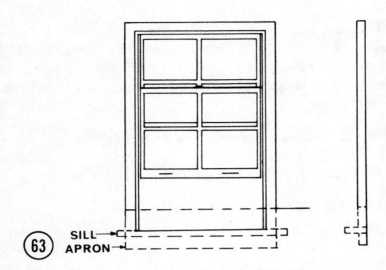

HOW TO HANDLE A LOW WINDOW

If you have a double hung window, 40″ or less from floor, here's what to do. Remove window apron, Illus. 63. Cut side window trim off at 40″ height. Saw sill off flush with wall. Cut three pieces of aluminum storm window channel length required to frame opening across bottom and sides. Slide a piece of frosted glass or plastic in place, Illus. 64. If window has handles on bottom rail, remove, and replace on side of window. The window will now slide behind frosted glass when in closed position. Close window. Fasten a piece of rubber weatherstripping across window to seal joint.

64

RADIATORS

Build base cabinets on both sides, connect with counter. Use this area to store a chair. If you need to increase circulation of warm air, cut a 4″ wide slot in counter. Cover slot with perforated aluminum.

If you prefer a soffit over wall cabinets; or wish to install a fluorescent fixture or luminous ceiling, etc., instructions are available in Book #694 Easi Bild Simplifies Electrical Repairs.

HOW TO REMOVE A DOOR OR WINDOW

Illus. 65, 66, indicates framing recommended for a door or window. If you want to remove a door or window and close opening, frame in with 2 x 4 studs 16″ on centers. If you want to cut a new opening, use 2-2x6, or 2-2x8, for header, Illus. 67. Your lumber dealer will provide size of rough opening required for door or window selected.

If you want to install gliding glass doors between kitchen and patio, complete step-by-step directions are provided in Book #613, How to Build and Enclose a Porch.

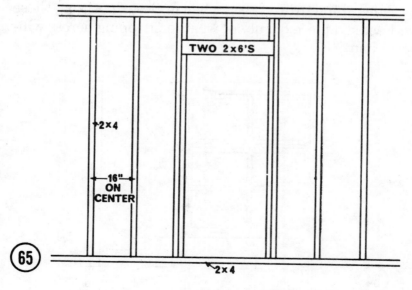

TWO 2x6'S

2x4

16″ ON CENTER

65

2x4

16″ —— 40.6 cm

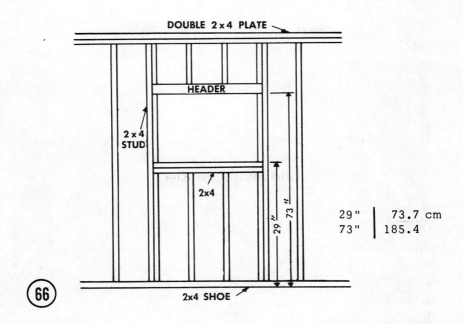

DOUBLE 2 x 4 PLATE

HEADER

2 x 4 STUD

2x4

| 29" | 73.7 cm |
| 73" | 185.4 |

2x4 SHOE

66

BUILD PASS THROUGH

Illus. 66 shows framing for a pass through between kitchen and dining area.

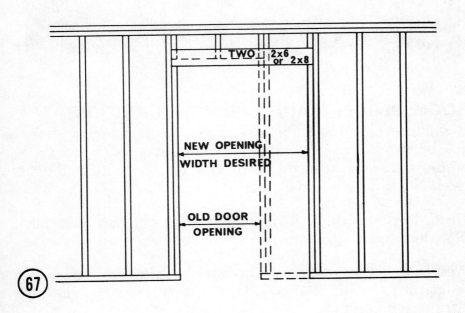

TWO 2x6 or 2x8

NEW OPENING WIDTH DESIRED

OLD DOOR OPENING

67

ROOM DIVIDERS AND CABINET FURNITURE

Building furniture and cabinets can provide pleasant and profitable hours of complete relaxation. For those seeking a part time business, there's a demand for this kind of built-in. Build one, use it as a sample to show others.

Read directions through completely before buying materials. Note location of each part in each illustration.

Wall-to-wall bookcases, cabinets and shelving from floor-to-ceiling, or to height desired, Illus. 68, can be built by following directions provided.

54

Free-standing room dividers, Illus. 69, containing any combination of components desired, can be built to fit space available. Wide spaced poles make this free-standing divider a sturdy storage unit.

Simplified construction permits building cabinets, drawers, magazine rack, desk unit, shelving, etc., Illus. 70, to fill your personal requirements.

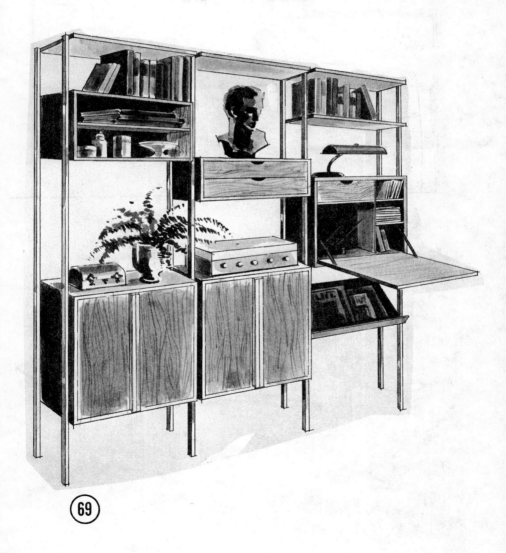

69

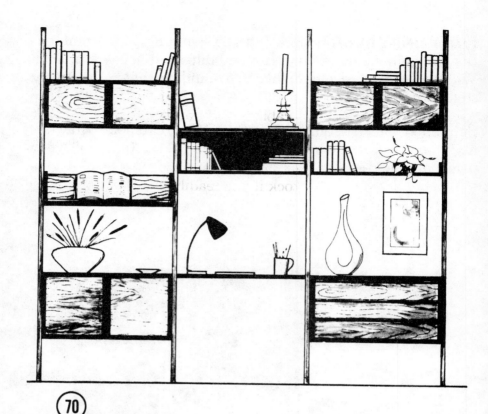

70

71

WALL INSTALLATION

A contemporary bedroom unit, Illus. 71, contains wardrobe with pull-out clothes hanger, make-up table, ample drawer unit, sliding door cabinets, plus a TV table or luggage stand. Plastic laminate on top of table, cabinet and vanity protects while it provides a professional finish.

All materials, from 1″ aluminum square tubing, Illus. 72, to hardwood paneling, are stock items readily available in lumber yards.

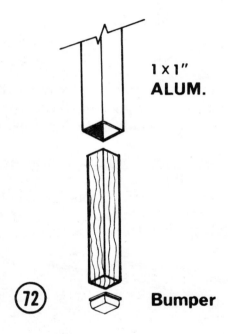

1 x 1″
ALUM.

(72)　　**Bumper**

To eliminate finishing, prefinished paneling is recommended. This requires no staining or waxing. It only requires gluing a paper-thin veneer to edge. If you build a unit that is to be painted, use fir plywood or flakeboard. Both come in 4x8 panels.

There are many different ways you can build cabinets. Top of cabinets can be covered with plastic laminate or with ¼″ prefinished paneling. Use ¾″ flakeboard for top of cabinet if it's to be covered with plastic laminate; use ½″ flakeboard for top of cabinet that's covered with ¼″ paneling.

Plastic laminate comes in a wide variety of colors and wood grains. Since it is easy to cement to flakeboard, you can cover top, sides and doors with professional results assured.

The ¾″ edge of a cabinet topped with plastic laminate can be finished with strips of laminate. The ¾″ edge of ¼″ prefinished paneling glued to ½″ flakeboard, can be covered with paper-thin matching veneer trim. This comes in rolls, in various wood grains, in width from 1″. Apply with white glue. Cut off surplus with a sharp knife or razor.

Cabinets built against a wall can be constructed with a single center pole, Illus. 68. Free-standing cabinets can be built with two poles, Illus. 69.

When building a cabinet for installation against a wall, Illus. 68, use ¼″ prefinished paneling with good face forward, when applying back to units containing book shelves or other open areas.

Use ¼″ prefinished paneling with good face exposed when applying backs to free-standing units. In free-standing units where opening is to be used for the display of small bric-a-brac, face inside of back with an additional piece of ¼″ paneling facing forward, Illus. 73.

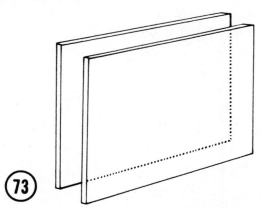

Cabinets built against wall can be fastened by nailing through back of cabinet into studs. Or these can be made free-standing by pressing legs firmly against ceiling, Illus. 74.

58

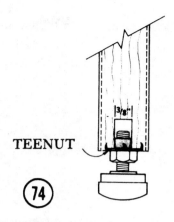

TEENUT

(74)

FLOOR TO CEILING INSTALLATION

When making a floor-to-ceiling installation, poles can be adjusted to fit snugly in position by following this procedure. Before inserting filler block, drill a ⅜″ hole to receive collar of a Teenut and shaft of bolt, Illus. 74. Drive a ¼″ Teenut in position, then drive block into leg. Insert a threaded dome of silence or use a ¼″ carriage bolt as an adjustable foot.

In rooms with acoustic, luminous or other types of dropped ceiling, or in cases where legs can't be secured by the adjustable foot, poles can be fastened to floor with a piece of 1″ angle, Illus. 75. To accurately locate position for angle bracket, place pole in position desired, mark floor, remove pole and screw angle to floor in position required. Replace pole. Drill through pole and angle bracket, fasten pole to bracket with self-tapping screw or rivet.

1″ square tubing comes in 6′ and 8′ lengths. Buy 8′ lengths for a floor-to-ceiling installation, buy 6′ or 8′ lengths for free-standing units.

Should your ceiling height be higher than 8′, you can add additional length by inserting a snug fitting block, Illus. 76, in top, and/or bottom, and allowing same to project amount required. Or you can use a filler block to reinforce a butt joint between two lengths of tubing. In this case, cut filler block to a size that permits applying epoxy glue.

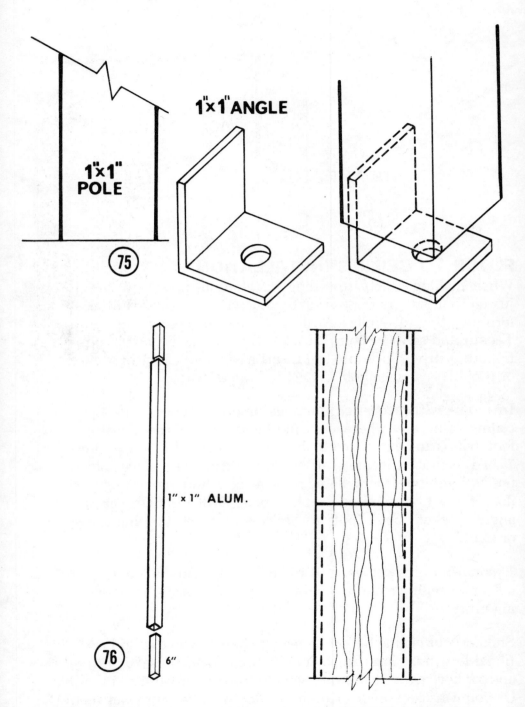

1"x1" POLE

1"x1" ANGLE

75

1" x 1" ALUM.

76

6"

Use self-sticking bumpers at exposed ends of filler blocks where same butt against ceiling.

(77)

All units, Illus. 77, consist of the following:

		Wide		Deep		High
A — Three drawer Cabinet		30″	x	16″	x	21″
B — Two drawer Vanity		30″	x	16″	x	6″
C — Sliding door Cabinet		30″	x	16″	x	14″
D — Sliding door Cabinet		30″	x	16″	x	18″
E — Wardrobe		30″	x	16″	x	60″
F — TV or Luggage Table		30″	x	16″	x	24″

Construction follows this procedure. Cut top, bottom and shelves same size, Illus. 78. Cut two ends and one back. Glue and nail ends to top and bottom. Check with square. Apply glue and nail back in position. Apply glue and nail ends and back to shelves. Doors can be hinged or installed with sliding door track as shown.

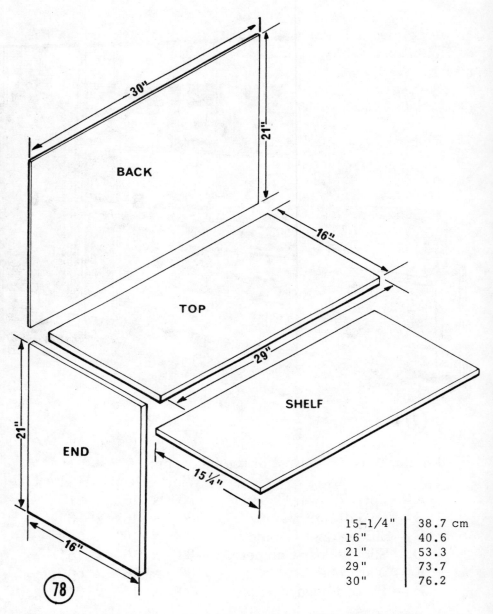

BACK

30"

21"

TOP

16"

29"

SHELF

END

21"

16"

15 1/4"

(78)

15-1/4"	38.7 cm
16"	40.6
21"	53.3
29"	73.7
30"	76.2

Before cutting ¼″ prefinished paneling, make a layout pattern. Cut all pieces for cabinet tops and other flat surfaces so grain is in position noted, Illus. 93.

Fasten assembled unit in position to poles by means of an expansion bolt, Illus. 79.

¼" prefinished paneling is glued in position. Plastic laminate is cut to full size of top and notched ¼" to fit around poles. Front edge of ¼" plywood and ½" flakeboard is covered with a paper thin veneer. Secure pole in position with adjustable foot, or fasten to floor with angle.

For a plastic laminate covered cabinet top, follow this procedure:

Cut ¾" flakeboard for top, bottom and shelves of Cabinet A, Illus. 77, to size indicated, Illus. 78, or to size desired. Cut ends from ½" flakeboard. Apply white glue, nail ends to top and bottom with 6-penny finishing nails. If unit is to be secured to wall, cut ¼" plywood to size required, glue and nail to back with good face forward. Cut shelves from ¾" flakeboard, glue and nail in position.

To simplify construction, build all units same depth.

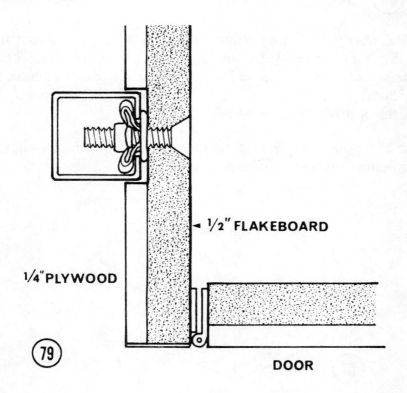

½" FLAKEBOARD

¼" PLYWOOD

79

DOOR

The first step is to measure space available, then divide by 28″, 30″ or 32″, to estimate number and width of units space will accommodate. Allow 1″ for each pole. Two poles plus one 30″ cabinet equals 32″. When space requires same, cabinets can be built less than 28″ or more than 32″ in width. Always build end cabinets equal width. Build middle cabinet to width required.

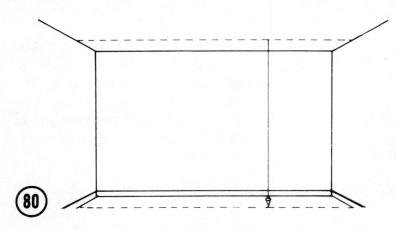

For center pole construction, measure 7⅝″ from wall, not from ceiling molding, and drop a plumb bob to floor, Illus. 80. Do this at both ends for a wall-to-wall cabinet. Snap a chalk line on floor, another on ceiling. This permits lining up poles in center of a 16″ cabinet.

For two pole construction, measure 2″ and 13″ from wall, snap chalk lines on floor and ceiling.

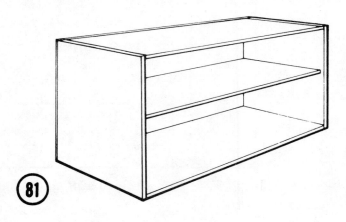

Cut shelves from ¾″ flakeboard or plywood, Illus. 81. Nail back and sides to shelf with 6-penny finishing nails. Stain shelf to match cabinet or paint color desired. Always install shelves before facing ends with ¼″ prefinished plywood.

When installing cabinets against a wall, place cabinet in position desired and mark wall. Drill hole and fasten cabinet temporarily with a 2″ screw into a stud. Check cabinet with level. Plumb it horizontally and vertically. Hold in position with 1x2's nailed temporarily to ends, Illus. 82. Expansion fasteners, Illus. 93, can also be used when you can't fasten to a stud.

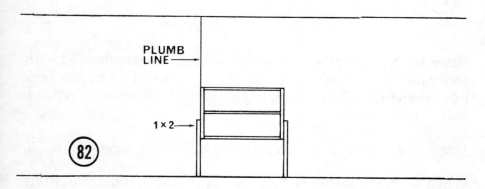

Cut 1″ aluminum square tubing to length required. Insert filler blocks, bumpers or adjustable feet to obtain length desired.

If cabinets are to be fastened to wall, locate studs. These are usually spaced 16″ on centers. Measure 16″ from corner and probe with a 6 penny finishing nail. When you have located one stud, draw lines on wall to indicate position of studs. Use a level vertically to guide you. Measure 16″ and try again. Draw lines sufficient length to guide you when fastening back of cabinet.

Drill one ¼″ hole thru end, in position required. Countersink hole to receive head of ¼″ No. 20 stove bolt, Illus. 79. Place pole in position, check with level to make certain it is plumb.

Indicate position of hole on pole. Using 7/16″ drill, bore hole in leg to receive jack nut, Illus. 83.

65

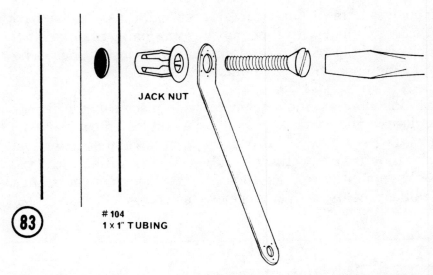

JACK NUT

#104
1 x 1″ TUBING

Place ¼″ No. 20 flathead bolt, Illus. 83, in holder supplied with jack nuts. Place jack nut in leg, tighten screw. This causes jack nut to expand. When completely expanded; Illus. 83, 84, remove bolt, remove holder.

Insert nut in pole, fasten in place by tightening screw, Illus. 83.

When securely fastened, remove screw and handle. Countersink hole, Illus. 79. Fasten end to pole, Illus. 85.

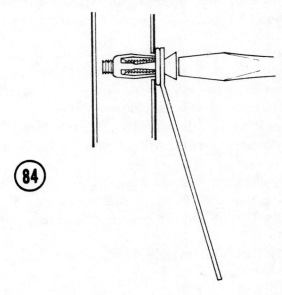

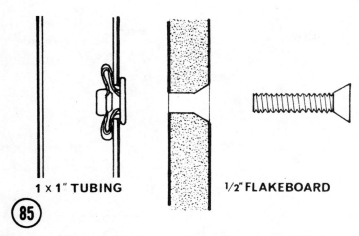

1 x 1″ TUBING   **1/2″ FLAKEBOARD**

(85)

Locate and drill a hole 2″ up from bottom, 8⅛″ from back of cabinet, for one pole, Illus. 68. Drill a ¼″ hole, countersink hole, Illus. 79. Place pole in position. Check pole with level in two directions. Mark and drill 7/16″ hole for a jack nut, Illus. 83. Follow jack nut installation procedure.

Fasten cabinet to pole with one screw. Check pole with level. Drill a second hole thru ½″ flakeboard end, 2″ down from top. Mark leg. Remove pole, drill hole for jack nut. Fasten pole permanently to end.

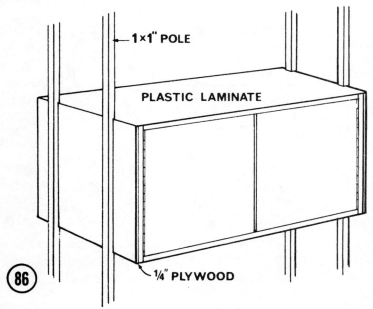

1×1″ POLE

PLASTIC LAMINATE

(86)   **¼″ PLYWOOD**

This procedure helps insure installing cabinets and poles plumb. Always tack 1x2 legs along outside edge of cabinet to allow space to fit poles in place. Follow this procedure when installing two poles in a free standing divider. Support cabinet with four 1x2 legs. Check with level. Use 1x2 legs until all poles have been attached.

To compensate for any variation in floor level, drill holes in poles after placing and plumbing same in position. You can tape pole to cabinet when marking hole location.

Cut ¼″ prefinished paneling to size required to face cabinet. Glue paneling to sides with panel adhesive. Cut plastic laminate to size required to cover top edge of ¼″ panel. Locate and notch laminate, Illus. 86, to fit snugly around pole. Use a file or saw. Apply contact cement to flakeboard and plastic laminate. Allow to set period prescribed by cement manufacturer. Carefully bond laminate to top.

Assemble end units to poles before fastening middle units. Fasten middle units by drilling thru sides and poles where it doesn't conflict with previously installed jack nuts.

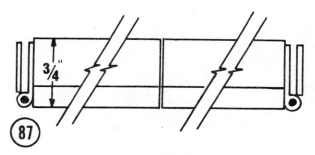

Hinged doors, Illus. 87, are made by cutting ½″ flakeboard to full size of opening. Cut ¼″ prefinished plywood same size. Glue ¼″ plywood to ½″ flakeboard, apply weight or clamps, allow to set period recommended by glue manufacturer. Saw in half to make two doors. Trim door to accommodate hinge. Fasten aluminum continuous hinge in position shown. The front edge of cabinet and exposed edges of door can be finished with paper thin veneer trim.

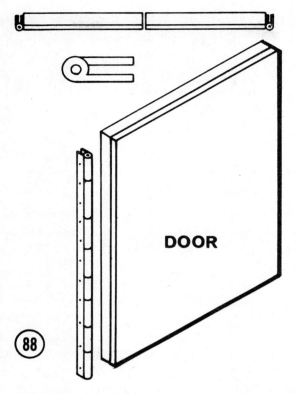

Cut aluminum continuous hinge to length of door. Fasten hinge to door, then to end, Illus. 88.

¼″ prefinished panels can be used for small sliding doors. Install with aluminum sliding door track, Illus. 89.

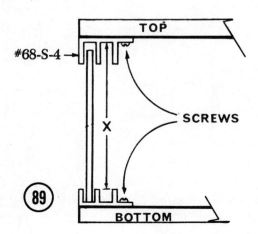

Fasten wide faced track in position at top, Illus. 89, narrow track in bottom. Cut panels ½ width of opening plus ½". This permits panels to overlap. Cut panels height of X, Illus. 89. Drill ¾" holes and install door pulls 1" from edge, center from top to bottom, Illus. 90.

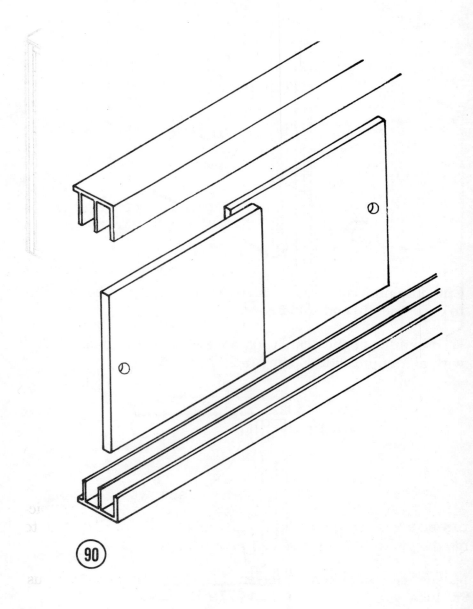

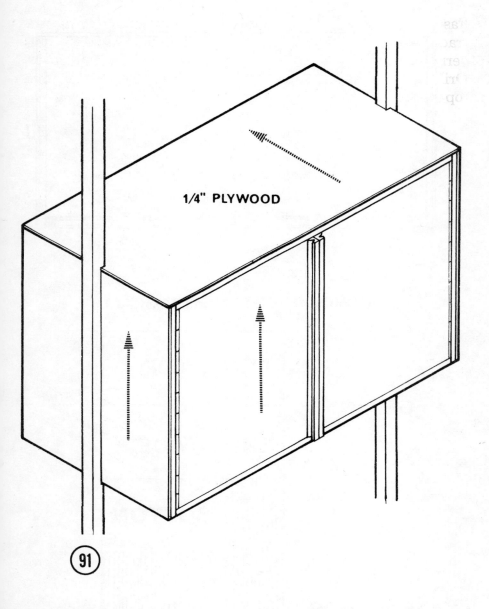

1/4" PLYWOOD

A full length door pull, Illus. 91, can be made from EB 23 picture molding. Drill holes thru door, apply glue, fasten door to molding with 1″ No. 6 flathead wood screws.

Magnetic catches can be fastened to door and to shelf, Illus. 92, 106.

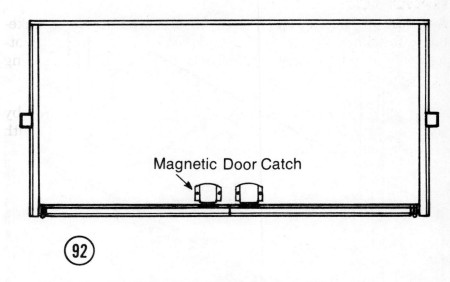

Magnetic Door Catch

(92)

PLYWOOD CUTTING DIAGRAM

GRAIN

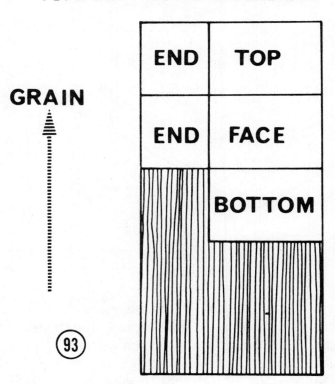

END	TOP
END	FACE
	BOTTOM

(93)

WARDROBE

A wardrobe, Illus. 94, can be built to size desired. Use ½″ flakeboard for sides, top and bottom. Cut sides 16x60, top and bottom 16″x24″ or to width desired. Use ¼″ prefinished paneling to face cabinet.

A top shelf can be cut full length and fastened in position by screwing into blocks inserted in poles, Illus. 72; or cut to width between poles and fastened with 1″ angle, Illus. 95.

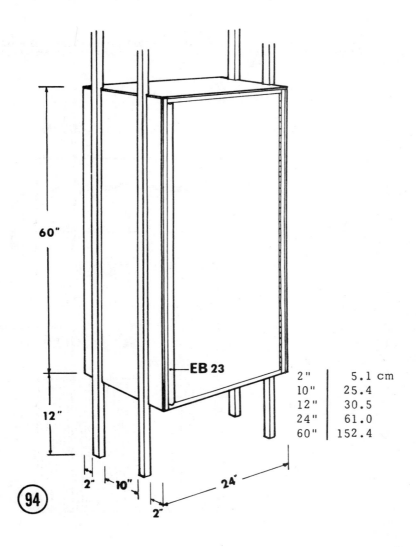

2"	5.1 cm
10"	25.4
12"	30.5
24"	61.0
60"	152.4

EB 23

94

Cut 1"x1" angle to length required to fit from pole to 1"x1" strip of wood fastened to wall. Cut wood strip same length as shelf. Nail strip to studs in wall. If you can't locate a stud, use expansion anchors, Illus. 25. Rivet or screw angle to pole at height desired. Drill holes in angle and fasten angle to shelf with ¾" No. 6 flathead wood screws.

Support for drawer B and table F, Illus. 77, for one pole.

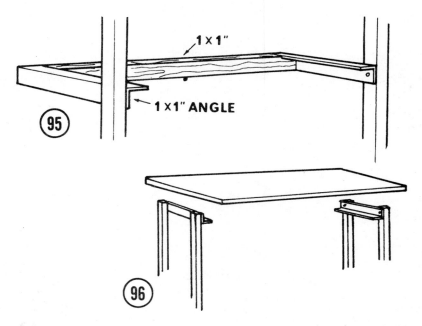

No wood strip is required on wall for two pole construction. Install ¼" prefinished paneling, good face down, when making top shelf or bottom of raised cabinets, Illus. 96.

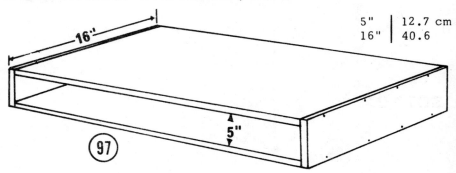

| 5" | 12.7 cm |
| 16" | 40.6 |

Use ½″ flakeboard for top, bottom and ends if top is to be covered with ¼″ prefinished paneling. Use ¾″ flakeboard if top is to be covered with plastic laminate, Illus. 97.

Cut sides, front and back 4⅝″ wide. Glue and nail front and back to sides. Glue and nail ¼″ bottom in position. Drill holes and fasten drawer pulls, Illus. 98, 99.

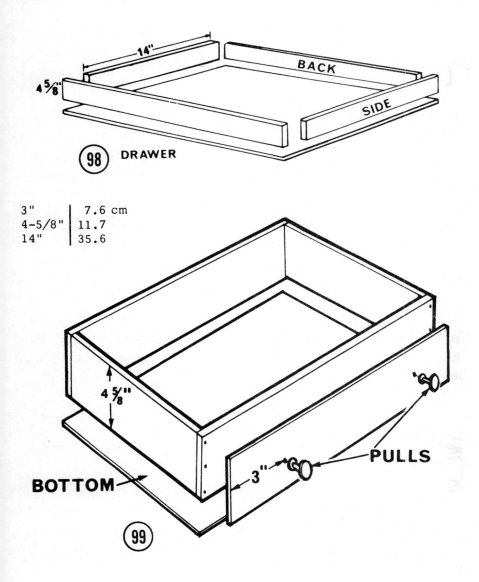

4⅝″

14″

BACK

SIDE

(98) DRAWER

3″	7.6 cm
4-5/8″	11.7
14″	35.6

4⅝″

PULLS

3″

BOTTOM

(99)

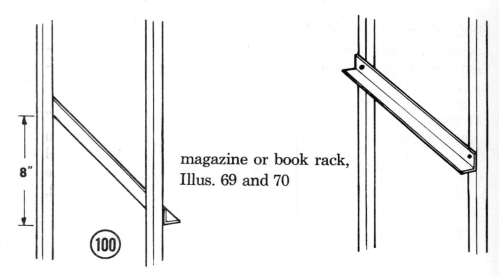

magazine or book rack,
Illus. 69 and 70

8″

MAGAZINE, BOOK RACK

A magazine or book rack, Illus. 100, can be fastened in place
with 1″ angle. Screw or rivet angle to pole in position noted, or
at angle and height preferred.

Cut ½″ flakeboard and ¼″ prefinished paneling to size required.
Glue together. Cut a piece of matching hardwood 1¾″ wide by
length required. Glue and nail hardwood in position noted,
Illus. 101.

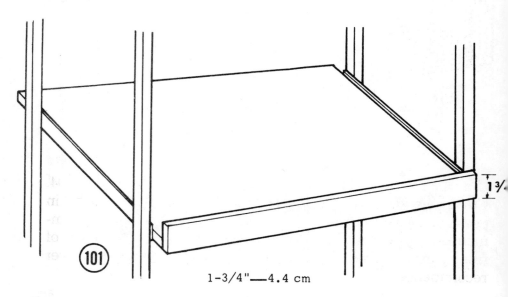

1-3/4″——4.4 cm

SPEAKER CABINETS

Speaker enclosure cabinets can be built any size speaker manufacturer specifies and installed in position that provides opti-
mum reception.

Glue and screw ¾"x¾" cleats V, Illus. 102, ¾" from back, ⅞"
from front. Staple 1" fiber glass blanket to sides, top and bottom
of cabinet between cleats. Cut ¾" flakeboard or plywood panel
to exact size required to fit snugly inside front and back. Place
back panel in position, mark area within cleats. Remove panel,
cut fiber glass to size, staple in position, Illus. 103.

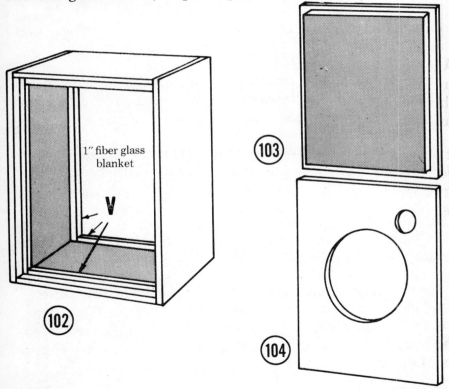

1" fiber glass blanket

Cut opening in front panel to size speaker requires, Illus. 104.
Cut a hole for vent pipe if same is recommended. Drill holes in
position speaker requires. Place rubber gasket or other recommended speaker seal in position and bolt speaker to inside of
front panel. Connect leads to speaker using wire manufacturer
recommends.

Cut acoustic fabric to sufficient size to cover front panel. Staple fabric to panel, Illus. 105.

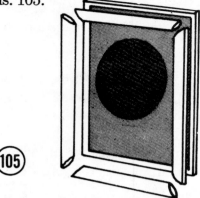

Drill hole through back or side in position required for speaker lead.

After fastening speaker enclosure to poles, fasten speaker panel to V using 1¼″ No. 6 flathead screws. Run speaker lead through hole and screw, do not glue, back panel in position.

Miter cut ⅜″x1¾″ molding to length required. Apply glue at corners. Nail in position to face of enclosure with 4 penny finishing nails. Countersink nailheads, fill holes with wood filler.

If you are building a wall installation, it will be necessary to screw back panel in position, fasten cabinet to poles, then fasten speaker panel last.

Fasten magnetic catch flush with edge of shelf with two screws placed in center of slot. Place door plate on magnet. Close door. Points on back of plate will indicate location on door. Fasten plate to door in position required. Reset catch to receive thickness of plate.

DOOR

SHELF

HOW TO BUILD CONVENTIONAL KITCHEN CABINETS

(106)

Conventional base and wall cabinets, Illus. 106, can be built to size specified, or length can be altered to fit space available. Step by step directions explain how to build a base cabinet measuring 30″ wide, 24″ deep, 36″ high.

Read directions through completely. Note each illustration and location of part mentioned. Always apply glue before nailing or screwing parts together, except when installing the cabinet to wall or floor. To compensate for any variance in sawcuts, lumber width, or thickness, always measure and cut parts to size required after you begin to assemble a cabinet, rather than size specified.

BASE CABINET

Cut two ¼″ plywood panels, 24″x36″, Illus. 107. Countertop fastens to top rail for a 36″ overall height. If you want a lower or higher base cabinet, cut to height desired. Notch bottom front 3″x3″.

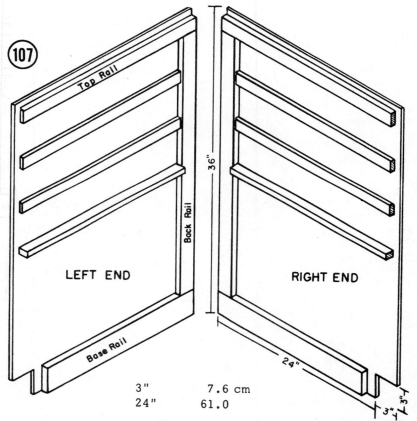

3″	7.6 cm
24″	61.0

Outside ends, Illus. 107, provide 3/4 recess for 3/4" countertop. Cut plywood sides 3/4" less in overall height, if you build a cabinet to fit <u>under</u> one long countertop, Illus. 111.

Cut two top rails, ¾ x 1¾ x 23¼″; four ½ x 1⅜ x 21½″ stop moldings; and two ¾ x 1¼ x 21½″ rails. Cut two base rails ¾ x 3 x 20″. Glue and nail top rail ¾″ down from top edge; one stop molding 6½″, 12¼″ and 18″, in position shown, Illus. 108. Cut two back rails, ¾ x 1¾ x 30½″. Nail in position.

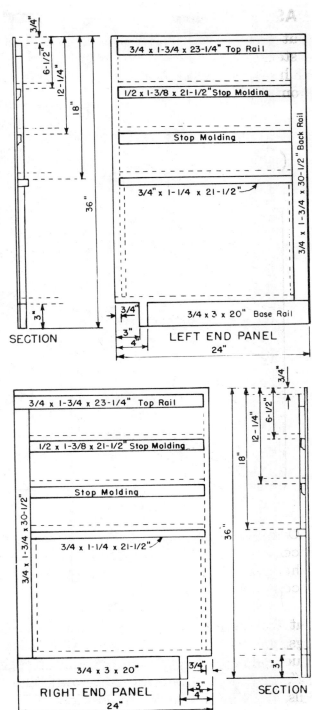

1/2"	1.27 cm
3/4"	1.91
1-1/4"	3.2
1-3/8"	3.5
1-3/4"	4.4
3"	7.6
4"	10.2
6-1/2"	16.5
12-1/4"	31.1
18"	45.7
20"	50.8
21-1/2"	54.6
23-1/4"	59.1
24"	61.0
30-1/2"	77.5
36"	91.4

SECTION

3/4 x 1-3/4 x 23-1/4" Top Rail

1/2 x 1-3/8 x 21-1/2" Stop Molding

Stop Molding

3/4" x 1-1/4 x 21-1/2"

3/4 x 1-3/4 x 30-1/2" Back Rail

3/4 x 3 x 20" Base Rail

LEFT END PANEL
24"

3/4 x 1-3/4 x 23-1/4" Top Rail

1/2 x 1-3/8 x 21-1/2" Stop Molding

Stop Molding

3/4 x 1-3/4 x 30-1/2"

3/4 x 1-1/4 x 21-1/2"

3/4 x 3 x 20"

RIGHT END PANEL
24"

SECTION

108

81

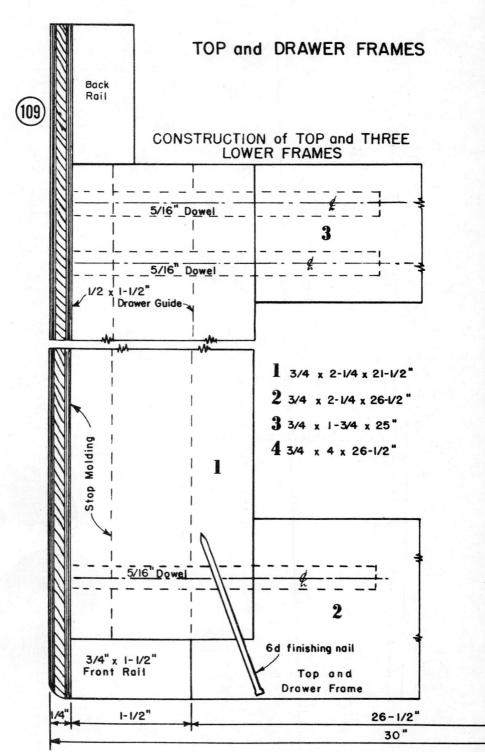

TOP and DRAWER FRAMES

Back Rail

(109)

CONSTRUCTION of TOP and THREE LOWER FRAMES

5/16" Dowel

3

5/16" Dowel

1/2 x 1-1/2" Drawer Guide

Stop Molding

1

1 3/4 x 2-1/4 x 21-1/2"
2 3/4 x 2-1/4 x 26-1/2"
3 3/4 x 1-3/4 x 25"
4 3/4 x 4 x 26-1/2"

5/16" Dowel

2

6d finishing nail

3/4" x 1-1/2" Front Rail

Top and Drawer Frame

1/4"   1-1/2"   26-1/2"

30"

1/4"	.64 cm		2-1/4"	5.7cm
1/2"	1.27		4"	10.2
3/4"	1.91		21-1/2"	54.6
1-1/4"	3.2		22-1/4"	56.5
1-1/2"	3.8		25"	63.5
1-3/4"	4.4		26-1/2"	67.2
			30"	76.2

BOTTOM FRAME

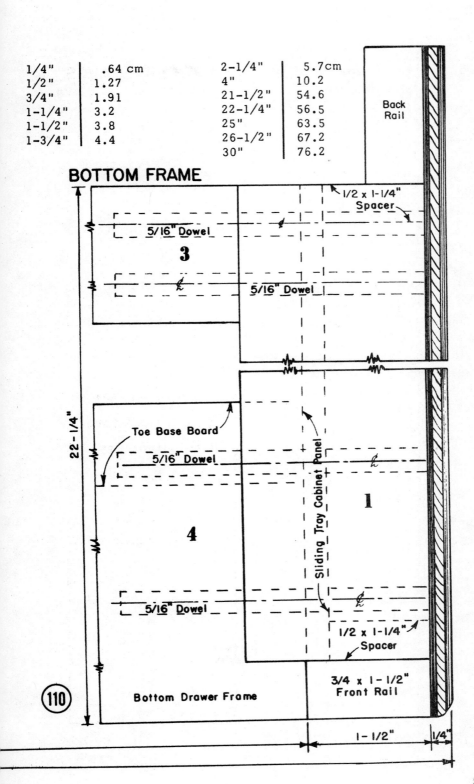

Back Rail

1/2 x 1-1/4" Spacer

5/16" Dowel

3

5/16" Dowel

Toe Base Board

5/16" Dowel

Sliding Tray Cabinet Panel

1

4

5/16" Dowel

1/2 x 1-1/4" Spacer

3/4 x 1-1/2" Front Rail

110

Bottom Drawer Frame

22-1/4"

1-1/2"   1/4"

Make bottom, drawer and top frames, Illus. 109, 110. Construction of bottom frame is shown on page 83. Construction of drawer and top frame is shown on page 82. To build cabinet to an overall width of 30″, do this. Buy clear 1x8 or 1x10 pine surfaced four sides and saw parts to size and length specified, or to size required to maintain overall dimensions shown.

Cut parts No. 1 — ¾ x 2¼ x 21½″
Cut parts No. 2 — ¾ x 2¼ x 26½″
Cut parts No. 3 — ¾ x 1¾ x 25″
Cut part No. 4 — ¾ x 4 x 26½″ for bottom frame.

To assemble bottom frame, cut one part #4, two parts #1, one part #3. Notch #4 to receive ¾ x 1½ front rail and #1. Clamp or temporarily nail all parts to a flat surface. Check frame with square. Drill ⁵⁄₁₆″ holes for dowels in position indicated, Illus. 110. Apply glue and drive dowels in position. Corner can also be joined with a 6 penny nail, Illus. 109, driven diagonally in position. Notch part #2 to receive part #1, Illus. 109, for top and drawer frames.

Build three drawer frames and one top frame using parts #1, 2, 3. Keep each frame clamped together until glue sets.

If you don't want to us dowels, apply glue and fasten with two ½″ corrugated fasteners into each joint.

You may prefer to cut notch for ¾ x 1½ front rail after assembling frames. Always cut notch to exact size of front rail.

To assemble cabinet, Illus. 111, cut ¾ x 3 x 29½″ toe board. Apply glue and nail to base rails. Nail sides to toe board.

Cut two ¾ x 1½″ front rails to length needed. Apply glue and nail sides to front rails in position shown.

Glue and nail front rail to bottom, drawer and top frames. Use 6 penny finishing nails. Check assembled frame with a square and hold square with 1 x 2 diagonal braces until glue has a chance to set.

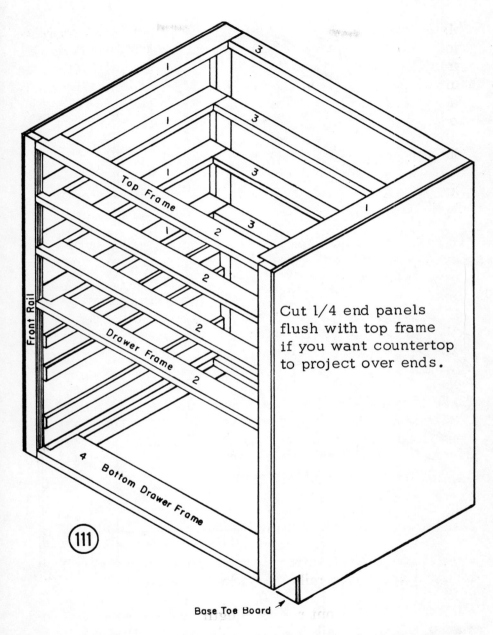

Cut 1/4 end panels
flush with top frame
if you want countertop
to project over ends.

Front Rail

Top Frame

Drawer Frame

Bottom Drawer Frame

(111)

Base Toe Board

Cut ½ x 1½ drawer guides, Illus. 112, and nail in position shown, Illus. 109.

Glue and nail ⅜ x 1⅜ x 21½″ stop molding to sides in position indicated, Illus. 111, 113. Note position of each stop molding.

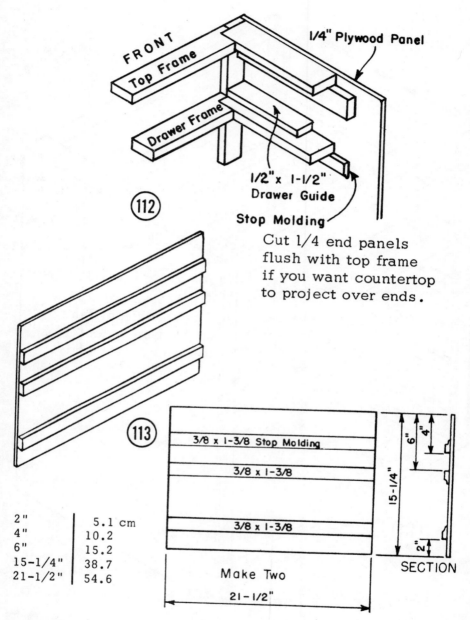

FRONT

Top Frame

Drawer Frame

1/4" Plywood Panel

1/2"x 1-1/2" Drawer Guide

Stop Molding

(112)

Cut 1/4 end panels
flush with top frame
if you want countertop
to project over ends.

(113)

3/8 x 1-3/8 Stop Molding

3/8 x 1-3/8

3/8 x 1-3/8

Make Two

21-1/2"

6"

4"

15-1/4"

2"

SECTION

2"	5.1 cm
4"	10.2
6"	15.2
15-1/4"	38.7
21-1/2"	54.6

Make drawers to size required. Cut sides ¾ x 4⅝ x 22¼"; back
¾ x 4⅝ x 25"; inner front panel ⅜ x 4⅝ x 25"; outer front panel
⅜ x 5¾ x 27¼", Illus. 114, 115, 116, 117. Cut bottom ¼ x 22¼ x
26½, Illus. 116. Cut ⅛ x 1 drawer slides, Illus. 114, full length of
bottom.

86

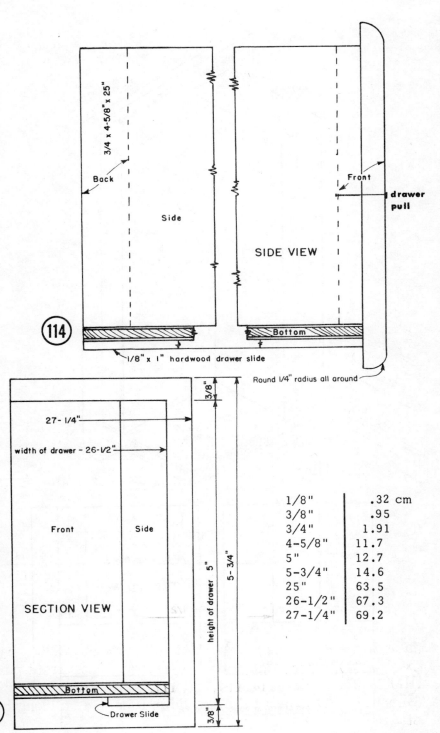

3/4 x 4-5/8 x 25"

Back

Side

SIDE VIEW

Front

drawer
pull

Bottom

(114)

1/8" x 1" hardwood drawer slide

Round 1/4" radius all around

3/8"

27-1/4"

width of drawer - 26-1/2"

Front   Side

SECTION VIEW

height of drawer 5"

5-3/4"

Bottom

Drawer Slide

3/8"

(115)

1/8"	.32 cm
3/8"	.95
3/4"	1.91
4-5/8"	11.7
5"	12.7
5-3/4"	14.6
25"	63.5
26-1/2"	67.3
27-1/4"	69.2

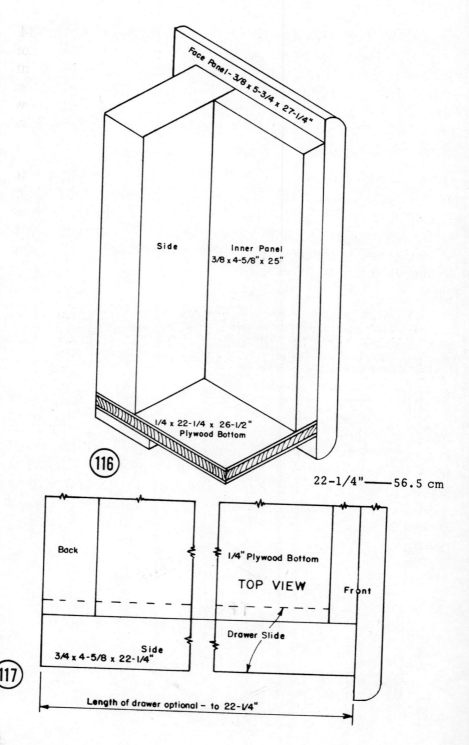

Face Panel - 3/8 x 5-3/4 x 27-1/4"

Side

Inner Panel
3/8 x 4-5/8" x 25"

1/4 x 22-1/4 x 26-1/2"
Plywood Bottom

(116)

22-1/4"——56.5 cm

Back

1/4" Plywood Bottom

TOP VIEW

Front

Side
3/4 x 4-5/8 x 22-1/4"

Drawer Slide

(117)

Length of drawer optional — to 22-1/4"

88

Round edges of outer drawer front to shape shown, Illus. 114, 117. The lipped edge extends ⅜″ at top, ½″ below bottom (or ⅜″ below slide). Glue and nail sides to back and inside front with 6 penny finishing nails. Glue and nail bottom to sides. Glue, do not nail, hardwood slide to bottom. Glue and screw inner front panel to outer panels using ⅝″ No. 7 flathead screws staggered about 6″ apart.

Make cabinet door, Illus. 118. Cut ⅜″ plywood inner panel to size of opening. Bevel edge ⅛″ on all four sides. Cut outer panel to project ⅜″ over framing on all four sides. Round edge of outer panel. Apply glue and fasten inner panel to outer panel with ⅝″ No. 7 screws. Place door in position. If necessary, plane top edge to fit it under lip on drawer.

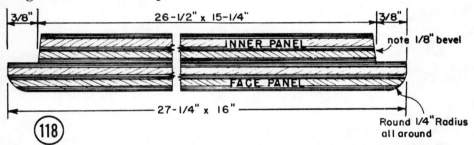

If you want to build storage trays for lower compartment, Illus. 119, cut tray front to shape shown, Illus. 119, 120. Miter cut trays sides, ¾ x 1¾ x 21½″. Cut front to shape shown, Illus. 120, ¾ x 1¾ x 26½″. Cut back to same size. Cut ¼ bottom to size required. Glue and brad sides to front and back, then nail to sides of tray. Nail ½ x 1¼ x 21½ and ½ x 1¼ x 14½ tray guides in position, Illus. 121.

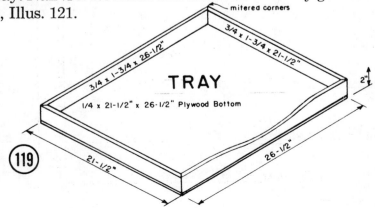

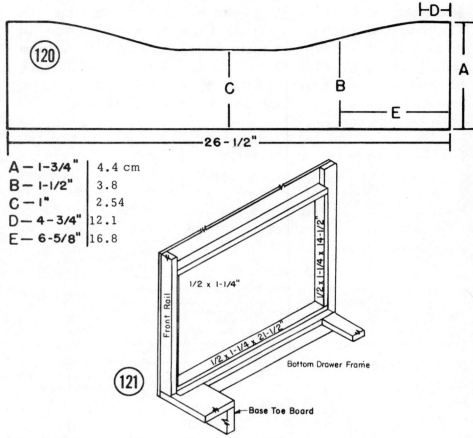

120

├─ D ─┤

A

C   B

├── E ──┤

├────────── 26-1/2" ──────────┤

A — 1-3/4"	4.4 cm
B — 1-1/2"	3.8
C — 1"	2.54
D — 4-3/4"	12.1
E — 6-5/8"	16.8

1/2 x 1-1/4"

1/2 x 1-1/4 x 14-1/2"

Front Rail

1/2 x 1-1/4 x 21-1/2"

Bottom Drawer Frame

121

← Base Toe Board

Install door in lower compartment with ⅜" semi-concealed offset hinges for a ¾" door. Place hinges 3" down from top, 3" up from bottom.

Fasten door and drawer pulls in position, Illus. 114, 2¾" down from top, 2¾" in from side.

⅞" plastic laminated countertops are available from most lumber retailers or you can make your own. Use ¾ exterior grade plywood and plastic laminate.

If cabinet is free standing, countertop can project 1" over ends and front. If cabinet butts against a sink, range or other cabinets, cut countertop flush with sides, only allow it to project 1" over front edge.

90

If a back splasher is used, cut to height desired. Nail or screw to countertop, Illus. 122. In this installation, cut counter 24¼ to obtain a 25″ overall width. If no back splasher is used, cut countertop 25″ in width. Apply plastic laminate using adhesive manufacturer recommends. Apply metal edging to top of back splasher and countertop. Apply a cove molding in position indicated.

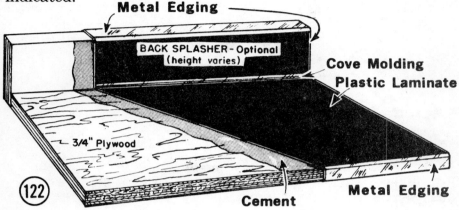

Metal Edging

BACK SPLASHER – Optional (height varies)

Cove Molding

Plastic Laminate

3/4″ Plywood

Cement

Metal Edging

If you don't want to remove a baseboard, Illus. 123, shows how to scribe a base cabinet to baseboard. Push base cabinet in position. Check cabinet with a level vertically as well as horizontally. Set scriber, Illus. 124, to distance of A. Draw line B. Using a jig or sabre saw, cut cabinet along B, Illus. 124, 125.

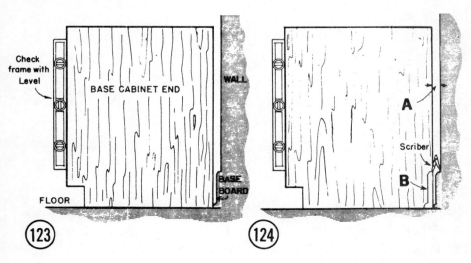

Check frame with Level

BASE CABINET END

WALL

BASE BOARD

FLOOR

A

Scriber

B

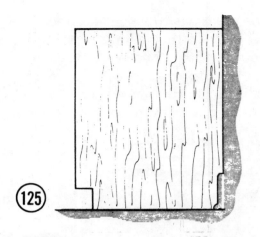

WALL CABINET

Wall cabinet construction, Illus. 126, 127, 128, follows the same general method used to build base cabinets. Cut ¼ x 12¾ x 32" side panels. Cut ¼ x 29½ x 31¼" back. Cut stop moldings and rails to size specified or size required.

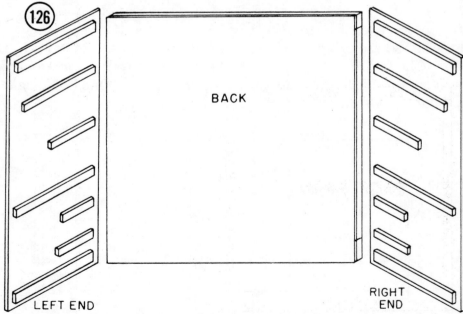

BACK

LEFT END

RIGHT END

Fasten shelf supports in position indicated, Illus. 127. Nail sides to back, top and bottom rails, Illus. 128. Cut and nail ¾" cabinet top and bottom to back and side rails.

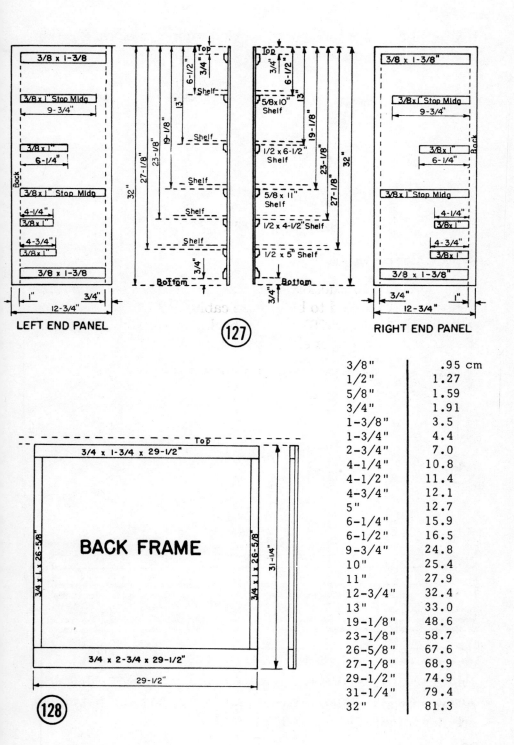

LEFT END PANEL

RIGHT END PANEL

BACK FRAME

3/8"	.95 cm
1/2"	1.27
5/8"	1.59
3/4"	1.91
1-3/8"	3.5
1-3/4"	4.4
2-3/4"	7.0
4-1/4"	10.8
4-1/2"	11.4
4-3/4"	12.1
5"	12.7
6-1/4"	15.9
6-1/2"	16.5
9-3/4"	24.8
10"	25.4
11"	27.9
12-3/4"	32.4
13"	33.0
19-1/8"	48.6
23-1/8"	58.7
26-5/8"	67.6
27-1/8"	68.9
29-1/2"	74.9
31-1/4"	79.4
32"	81.3

93

Use ½″ plywood or flakeboard for wall cabinet shelves. Position of shelves is optional, Illus. 129, 130.

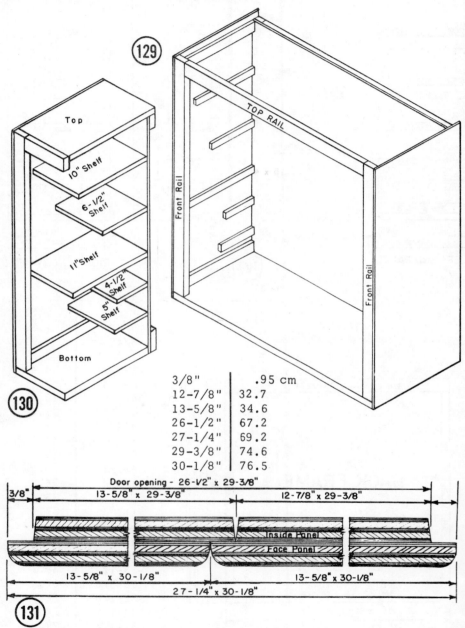

3/8″	.95 cm
12-7/8″	32.7
13-5/8″	34.6
26-1/2″	67.2
27-1/4″	69.2
29-3/8″	74.6
30-1/8″	76.5

A pair of wall cabinet doors, Illus. 131, should be made to fit opening. Again allow a ⅜″ lip all around.

Door racks, Illus. 132, are optional. These can be cut to shape and fastened in position shown, Illus. 133, or in position desired.

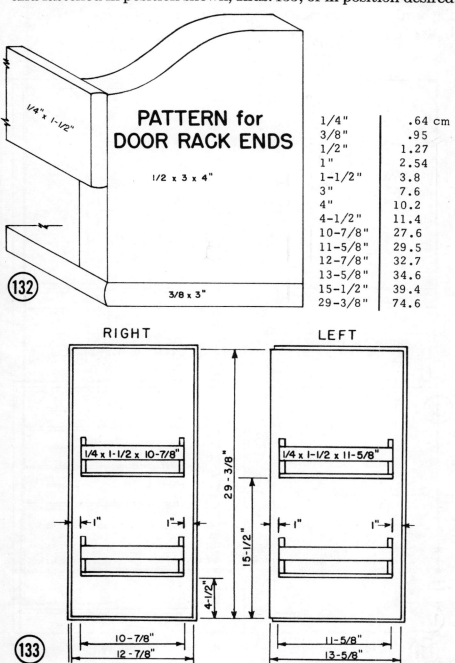

PATTERN for DOOR RACK ENDS

1/2 x 3 x 4"

1/4" x 1-1/2"

3/8 x 3"

1/4"	.64 cm
3/8"	.95
1/2"	1.27
1"	2.54
1-1/2"	3.8
3"	7.6
4"	10.2
4-1/2"	11.4
10-7/8"	27.6
11-5/8"	29.5
12-7/8"	32.7
13-5/8"	34.6
15-1/2"	39.4
29-3/8"	74.6

RIGHT   LEFT

1/4 x 1-1/2 x 10-7/8"   1/4 x 1-1/2 x 11-5/8"

29 - 3/8"

15-1/2"

4-1/2"

1"   1"   1"   1"

10-7/8"   11-5/8"
12 - 7/8"   13-5/8"

95

Fill all nail and screw holes with wood filler. Prime coat before painting. Wall cabinet is fastened to studs in wall with 2″ No. 8 flathead wood screws. Most wall cabinets are fastened 16″ above base counter, Illus. 134.

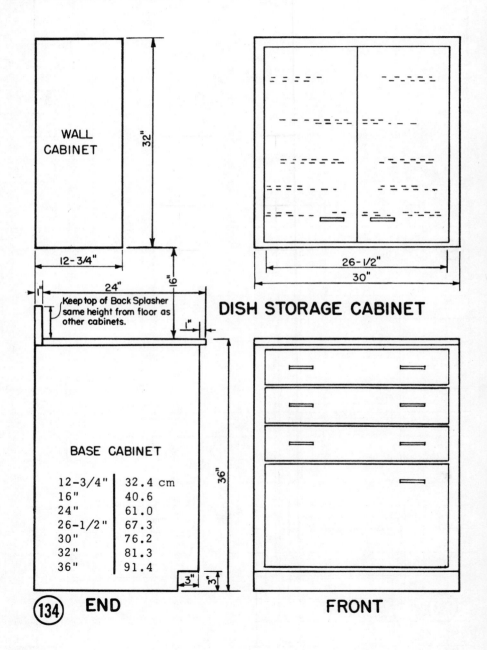

WALL CABINET

32″

12-3/4″

24″

16″

Keep top of Back Splasher same height from floor as other cabinets.

1″

1″

DISH STORAGE CABINET

26-1/2″

30″

BASE CABINET

12-3/4″	32.4 cm
16″	40.6
24″	61.0
26-1/2″	67.3
30″	76.2
32″	81.3
36″	91.4

36″

3″

3″

(134) END

FRONT

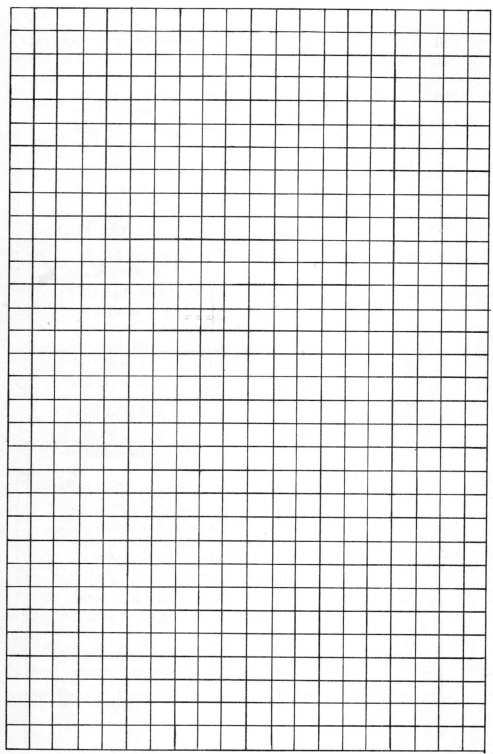

HOW TO THINK METRIC

Government officials concerned with the adoption of the metric system are quick to warn anyone from attempting to make precise conversions. One quickly accepts this advice when they begin to convert yards to meters or vice versa. Place a metric ruler alongside a foot ruler and you get the message fast.

Since a meter equals 1.09361 yards, or 39⅜" +, the decimals can drive you up a creek. The government men suggest accepting a rough, rather than an exact equivalent. They recommend considering a meter in the same way you presently use a yard. A kilometer as 0.6 of a mile. A kilogram or kilo as just over two pounds. A liter, a quart, with a small extra swig.

To more fully appreciate why a rough conversion is preferable, note the 6" rule alongside the metric rule. A meter contains 100 centimeters. A centimeter contains 10 millimeters.

As an introduction to the metric system, we used a metric rule to measure standard U.S. building materials. Since a 1x2 measures anywheres from ¾ to ²⁵⁄₃₂ x 1½", which is typical of U.S. lumber sizes, the metric equivalents shown are only approximate.

Consider 1" equal to 2.54 centimeters;
10" = 25.4 cm.
To multiply 4¼" into centimeters: 4.25 × 2.54 = 10.795 or 10.8 cm.